RICHMOND'S
CULINARY HISTORY

RICHMOND'S
CULINARY HISTORY

SEEDS OF CHANGE

Maureen Egan & Susan Winiecki

Foreword by Dr. Leni Sorensen

AMERICAN PALATE

Published by American Palate
A Division of The History Press
Charleston, SC
www.historypress.net

Front cover, top right: Richmond Dairy at Marshall and Jefferson Streets. *Cook Collection, The Valentine.*

First published 2017

Manufactured in the United States

ISBN 9781467138154

Library of Congress Control Number: 2017945027

*To our husbands, who put up with our bits (OK, piles) of paper
and to the memory of Lillian W. Raible, who taught* Winesburg, Ohio,
and much more

CONTENTS

CONTENTS

FOREWORD

Dear Reader,

I'm not gonna take too much of your time here, as I want you to get right to the topic at hand: Richmond and food and history and a rich assortment of folks exhibiting incredible pluck and bravery and gumption, not to mention great cooking and entrepreneurial spirit! The stories Maureen and Susan are sharing here are not run-of-the-mill civic boosterism—the "ain't our city grand?" successes.

No, we've got a dynamic woman who insisted on creating clubs to teach girls home economics in the early twentieth century while herself participating in the suffragist movement, the ultimate winning of the women's vote and the founding of the Virginia League of Women Voters. There is the self-emancipated chef and caterer who insisted on paying his former owner to the last penny for his freedom but who also confided a core truth in his day to his son: "All your books haven't taught you never to let a white man know how much you really know about anything except hard work."

The James River is a major character with its eighteenth- and nineteenth-century flour mills clustered along its banks sending flour around the world and the river's history of the ancient sturgeon once plentiful, then nearly driven to extinction and now, after much community effort, a proud resident again. There's an unexpected metal industry, there is a warehouse full of exotic spices and they are side by side with cozy tearooms, box lunch restaurants that still have loyal customers lining up out the doors and lunch counters in fancy department stores where African American students won their rights to be served. These stories offer us a Richmond that many do not know but all will be the better for knowing.

Leni Sorensen, PhD
Culinary Historian
Crozet, Virginia

PREFACE

*During the winter he read to her all of the odds and ends of thoughts he had
scribbled on the bits of paper. After he had read them he laughed and stuffed them
away in his pockets to become round hard balls.*
—Sherwood Anderson, "Paper Pills"

This book reminds us of all the scribbled, stuffed-away notes that Dr.
Reefy in *Winesburg, Ohio* was finally able to share with someone who
truly cared.

Since the fall of 2010, we have walked Richmond's neighborhoods, giving
food tours that weave together history, neighborhood news and culinary
highlights. We've planned dining events that draw from our city's past while
making contemporary connections. Through each tour and event, we have
gathered notes and tucked them away. This book represents the unfurling of
our paper pills.

Our book isn't a history of Richmond restaurants and how they got their
names but, rather, a tale in chapters of how our city has changed over four
hundred years through the lens of food and its makers.

Richmond is a complex place, always deserving of a better telling of its
story through voices that often weren't heard and well documented—the
voices of Native Americans, the voices of free and enslaved blacks, the
voices of women and the voices of immigrants and other outsiders. We try
to offer those.

We also try to share the stories of some of its firsts—the first truly regional cookbook, the first technical education classes, the first test market for aluminum foil and the first manufacturer to package extracts for the consumer.

Through naturalization papers, census records, scribbled drawings, hefty scrapbooks and the help of the city's giving reference librarians, we have pieced together stories of some amazing Richmond characters you may be reading about for the first time. For others, we hope that you get to know them a little better. Some of our subjects knew how to work a system they found themselves in to their best advantage. Others set their own brave course. All were marketers extraordinaire in their own right, using everything from recipes for turtle soup to customer testimonials to turn heads or change minds.

Anderson used twenty-two stories to paint a portrait of the small town of Winesburg; we use twenty-four chapters to paint ours of Richmond. And we've already started collecting more bits of paper for the next.

ACKNOWLEDGEMENTS

We hesitate to write this section, as we fear both never getting to the end of our thank-yous and leaving out someone who deserves our appreciation. Let's start with the Richmond food and drink community, which has embraced and supported our food tours and other events with its cheery collaborative nature and enthusiasm. We're grateful you keep letting us in! And thanks so much to those who have walked with us around town—in person or on Twitter—who are as curious as we are and as fascinated by the tales Richmond has to tell. We feel a debt of gratitude to the people whose stories we tell. Through it all, we've learned about the persuasive power of turtle soup—especially the version served in Richmond by Anna Cora Mowatt to Virginia legislators, who, in turn, voted to allow women to incorporate businesses in 1856. And we learned that there was absolutely nothing dainty about the women who served dainties in Richmond.

To the keepers of so many stories—the Valentine, the Black History Museum and Cultural Center, the Virginia Historical Society, VCU's James Branch Cabell Library's Special Collections and Archives, the Richmond Public Library's Main Branch and the Library of Virginia—we'd be lost without you and your attentive staffs. Thanks, too, to our co-workers at all of our ventures. Thank you for understanding that the glazed look in our eyes wasn't due to lack of interest in what you were saying but from another late-night deadline. And finally, a heartfelt thank-you to our families, especially our husbands, who have heard us go on about this quirky discovery and that little-known pioneer but haven't heard us say thank you often enough. Thank you all for everything. We mean it!

CHAPTER 1

THE THREE SISTERS AND THE CHIEF

Virginia Indians' Influence

Much of what passes for culinary trends today—farm-to-table, nose-to-tail, eating local, eating seasonally—was embedded in the culture of the Native American tribes that lived in the area that is now Virginia for thousands of years before Spanish and English explorers arrived. When the English came ashore in 1607 near present-day Jamestown, they set foot on Powhatan's land. Powhatan was the paramount chief of multiple tribes that lived from the Chesapeake Bay to the Falls of what was then known as the Powhatan River (now the James) and northward to the Potomac River. You might know him as the father of Pocahontas as well.

When he became leader in the late sixteenth century, the tribes he reigned over included the Pamunkey, Arrohattoc, Mattaponi, Appomattoc, Powhatan and Youghtanund, all within fifty miles of the Falls. He eventually expanded his loose confederation to more than two dozen tribes. Historians estimate that up to twenty thousand Native Americans lived in villages along waterways within Powhatan's chiefdom.[1]

DELAYED RECOGNITION

Over the centuries, new colonists and authorities used violence, trickery and neglect to try to erase the native people from Virginia. The Racial Integrity Act of 1924 used unadulterated racism to make it illegal for anyone in Virginia to identify oneself as Indian. Decades of obliterating Indians from the state's ledgers had a dastardly effect on the Virginia tribes, making it that much harder to transmit cultural knowledge. The law was overturned by the U.S. Supreme Court finally in 1967. Today, Virginia's tribes enroll approximately 3,500 people officially, though it's likely that thousands more are eligible. It was only in 2016 that the Pamunkey, who count among their forebears both Powhatan and his daughter Pocahontas, became the first Virginia tribe to gain federal recognition. The others are still waiting.[2]

Virginia Indian tribes still haven't received recognition for their contributions to Virginia foodways. Foraging and farming, hunting and fishing, all were integral to the Powhatan culture. The English colony would not have survived "the starving time" had the Native Americans not shared their foodways with the colonists.

VIRGINIA HOSPITALITY

It was Powhatan Indians who welcomed John Smith, Christopher Newport and Gabriel Archer and crew as they explored the James River soon after landing in Jamestown in 1607. The Englishmen were hoping to find passage to China but instead stopped at one of Chief Powhatan's three tribal homes near today's Fulton Hill at the east end of what is now Richmond and were welcomed by the chief's son, Parahunt. Smith noted that along the river, "with many fresh Springes, the people in all places kindely intreating us, daunsing and feasting us with strawberries, Mulberies, Bread, Fish, and other their Countrie provisions wherof we had plenty."[3] Young Powhatan boys showed the English how they dove for mussels. A feast with venison ensued. The colonists provided the liquor.

On Fulton Hill overlooking the river, Smith and company noted a dozen homes and paths leading east and west. Fields were located near the village, and the hosts instructed the English in planting corn.

As farming was considered women's work in Powhatan culture, it's no surprise that their favorite crops—corn, beans and squash—would be called the "three sisters." Using wooden digging sticks, the women would dig holes in the roughly cleared ground between tree stumps and plant corn and beans in the same hole, with squash nearby. The cornstalk acted as a ladder for the beans to climb, and the squash covered the ground, keeping down weeds. Oftentimes, a fourth sister would be welcomed, as sunflowers provided useful seeds and shade to keep the crops from drying out. English visitors noted that the Indians planted four kinds of corn—two that ripened

A Virginia Indian village with homes and fields adjacent, circa 1590. *Theodor de Bry, engraver, and John White, artist, Library of Congress.*

in early summer, and flint corn and she-corn that ripened late. Apparently, the juice from green cornstalks was as sweet as cane juice.[4]

Corn was more than a staple of the Native American garden and diet; it was wealth, for it was the key to the tribes' year-round sustenance. The women harvested and dried some of the corn that would be worked by hand and stone into cakes. In fact, the name of the Chickahominy, another of Virginia's tribes, means "people of the coarse pounded corn." The colonist George Percy noted, "After they pound their [grain] into flowre with hote water, they make it into a paste, and worke it into round balls and Cakes, then they put it into a pot of seething water....When it is sod thoroughly, they lay it on a smooth stone, there they harden it as well as in an Oven."[5]

Percy said native women "doe all their drugerie," including farming, building shelters and making tools and baskets out of animal bones, sticks, stones and shells. The women foraged for nuts, berries, roots and plants.[6]

FISHING AND HUNTING

The Indians congregated near rivers for the food and, in the case of the town near the Falls, for the tool-making resource the rocks and churning river provided. Indeed, the word "Powhatan" roughly translates to "current in water." Shad and herring coming up the river to spawn in the spring gave the men and boys the chance to show their skills as they caught them with fish weirs made of sticks or with arrows tied to strings. Large sturgeon roamed the James back then, sometimes caught in fresh water by lassoing.[7]

The natives were canoe-oriented, making huge dugout canoes that could hold thirty men and their belongings. Smoked and dried fish and oysters were important protein sources on such journeys. Large middens, towers of oyster shells, in tidal rivers east of Richmond attest to the popularity of oysters centuries ago. Shellfish in bisque thickened with cornmeal and fish boiled in stew were both considered noteworthy by early colonial journal-keepers.[8]

John Smith's notes make it clear that the native women had many styles of preparing foods:

> *Their fish and flesh they boyle either very tenderly, or broyle it so long on hurdles over the fire, or else, after the Spanish fashion, putting it on a spit, they turne first the one side, then the other, till it be as drie as their jerkin Beefe in the West Indies, that they may keepe it a month or more without putrefying. The broth of fish or flesh they eate as commonly as the meat.[9]*

The roasting technique of tribes native to Virginia, as John Smith and others have noted. *Theodor de Bry, engraver, and John White, artist, Library of Congress.*

Hunting was men's work and could entail stalking while dressed as a deer or trapping smaller animals such as beaver and otter. Deer were the prize catch, pursued by tracking the signs of the forest with bow and arrow or with a large contingent of hunters or by setting fires to encircle a herd and letting fly when an exhausted creature bound out of the fire line. Other worthy targets were wild turkeys, rabbits, ducks, partridges and geese.[10]

The women's cooking techniques for venison varied with the circumstances. Sometimes the meat would be dried in smoke or boiled or roasted. Later in the seventeenth century, the preparation of food that was "barbcuted, that is wrapped up in leaves and roasted in embers," appealed to some, while a stew with deer brains and entrails got a rave review from at least one colonist.[11]

Once a year, those who lived farther to the east picked up stakes and headed for a large-scale hunt near the Falls, with the women handling meal preparation and housekeeping by bringing along dried meats and corn, pots and utensils. Though the village Smith and company visited in 1607 sat on high ground overlooking the river, digging in 1974 for a development in Shockoe Slip turned up signs of a Native American settlement next to the river, including pieces of pottery, seeds and animal bones.[12]

TRIBUTES GO BOTH WAYS

Pamunkey chief George Cook presents the annual tribute of local game at the Executive Mansion during the visit of President William Taft on November 22, 1910. *Library of Virginia.*

Both the Pamunkey and the Mattaponi have reservations along the eponymous rivers today because of seventeenth-century treaties. The rivers still provide them sustenance, as both tribes built fish hatcheries to help continue their fishing traditions and restore the shad population after years of decline. According to a Virginia Foundation for the Humanities radio interview with Todd Custalow, a member of the Mattaponi, the tribe built its first fish hatchery in 1917 to help preserve the shad population along the river that is so integral to the tribe's culture. As Custalow said, "I firmly believe that our hatcheries… helped our rivers sustain the shad run and the shad population. You can't just keep taking, and taking, and taking from the river. You gotta put back and that way there will be fish there for future generations."[13]

Though the Pamunkey and Mattaponi still haven't received the recognition they deserve for their crucial contributions to American culture in general and Virginia foodways in particular, they still honor 1646 and 1677 treaties and present the Annual Tax Tribute on the fourth Wednesday in November to the governor at Capitol Square in Richmond. Originally, the treaty called for twenty beaver pelts to be sent to the English king. Over the centuries, the tribute has evolved to include deer, strings of rockfish, ducks, partridges or turkeys, presented to the governor in a colorful and dignified ceremony. It's unfortunate that Native American contributions to American cuisine are given a nod around Thanksgiving and largely ignored the rest of the year. Virginia foodways and Virginia hospitality have their roots in the Powhatan Indian tribes' rich cultures, and there's so much more to be discovered, acknowledged and honored.

CHAPTER 2

RING THE BELL

Sixth Street Market

James W. Rouse, the developer of Harborplace in Baltimore, Faneuil Hall in Boston and Waterside in Norfolk, the man who declared in 1981 that the American city was being reborn, came to Richmond to build not a mall but a festival marketplace.[14]

In April 1981, Rouse and his wife founded Enterprise Foundation, a nonprofit concentrating on partnerships with community groups that would address affordable housing and services for poor neighborhoods. The foundation was to be funded in part by Rouse's for-profit Enterprise Development Co.[15]

Through Enterprise Development Co., Rouse wanted to create an urban shopping destination with a food court, sit-down restaurants and shops that spanned Broad Street, leading on the southern end to two major downtown department stores, Miller & Rhoads and Thalhimers, and to the historic 1910 Richmond Blues Armory on the northern end.[16]

Rouse was angling to name the marketplace The Bridge; however, Clarence L. Townes Jr., a member of the racially diverse sixty-person Richmond Renaissance group that collaborated on the project, won out with the name 6th Street Marketplace—a tip of the hat to the market vendors and stalls that once ran along Sixth, north of Broad Street three blocks to Clay Street. An old photo of the Sixth Street Market hanging in the Miller & Rhoads executive suites that Rouse spotted when in town for a meeting sealed the deal on the name.

A 1930s view of Sixth Street Market from Broad Street with the Blues Armory on Marshall in background. *The Valentine.*

"I can still remember the smell of the flowers, meat and vegetables in the 1940s and 1950s," Townes told Shelley Rolfe of the *Richmond Times-Dispatch* in 1984. "I can remember selling the *Afro-American* at the Sixth Street Market. I sold so many I won a trip to the 1940 New York World's Fair."[17]

SECOND ON SIXTH

The Sixth Street Market, also called Second or New Market, was established in 1817 on the southeast corner of Marshall and Sixth Streets, some twenty-five years after First or Old Market was placed at Seventeenth and Main Streets in Shockoe Bottom.[18]

By 1853, Second Market had expanded north of Marshall with a building bearing a brick loggia at the south end that held a police station. A belfry on top of the station contained a seven-hundred-pound bell used to open and close the market and to sound alarms. A fish market was added in 1856.[19]

First Market at Seventeenth and East Franklin Streets in Shockoe Bottom. *Cook Collection, The Valentine.*

The city also built in 1886 a "new" Second Market—the Sixth Street Meat Market—on the site of the original 1817 market. In the late 1890s, ads still referred to the area as Second Market. By the early 1920s, however, the public referred to it solely as Sixth Street Market.[20]

But Sixth Street Market began struggling in the 1950s. The city's streetcar system was abolished in 1949, and automobiles made trips to burgeoning supermarket chains easy. By 1956, the city was eyeing the site of the 1886 Meat Market for a new parking deck for downtown shoppers, and by 1964, it came down and the deck went up. Two of the market's ornamental bull's heads were placed at the Seventeenth Street Market.[21]

The brick bays of the Richmond Blues Armory continued to be used as market vendor space until the city and Rouse came up with the design for 6th Street Marketplace and enclosed the Armory space.

The September 18, 1985 opening of the nearly $30 million 6th Street Marketplace came with a parade, glowing newspaper editorials and a "smorgasbord of specialty foods," including The Fudgery, where employees rang a bell when fudge was ready for sale and consumption.[22]

William Wood, Sixth Street Market vendor, circa 1907. *Library of Congress.*

A SYMBOL

"In addition to providing jobs, the marketplace project is expected to generate some $1.5 million in tax revenue the first year alone," opening organizer Thomas H. Park told Carol A.O. Wolf of *Style Weekly* the week before the opening. "The marketplace will become the symbol for downtown. The bridge linking both sides of Broad Street is especially important because it shows that the black and white communities are reaching out to one another."[23]

Rouse pulled out of the project by February 1988, saying that he had invested $2 million more than what he perceived as his company's obligation. He explained his departure to *Richmond Times-Dispatch* reporter Rob Walker while having two dry martinis at the Marriott.[24]

The city, along with a vexing array of partners, operators and managers, tried to keep the marketplace afloat. By 1996, according to the *Richmond Free Press*, the mall had lost more than $20 million and still required an annual city subsidy of $1.3 million to remain open.[25]

Almost thirty years after opening, most of the marketplace and bridge were demolished in October 2003 to make way for the next thing touted to revitalize downtown: a performing arts complex, yet another private-public partnership with a confusing tangle of partners, operators and managers funded with an increase in the city's meals tax that still remains.

CHAPTER 3

MILLERS TO THE WORLD

Flour's Power

Walking along Richmond's riverfront today, you're likely to see kayakers and rafters rush through the white water as families exult over the roar of the rapids under the Tyler Potterfield Memorial Bridge. On the tidal portion of the James not far to the east, herons pose, folks fish in boats or off bridges and paddle boarders and rowers ply the current. Look closely, though, and you can see signs of industry that once made the city a port of international importance—a millrace here, a canal lock there.

The James River's drop of 107 feet in seven miles produces thrills and spills now and once powered grinding stones to pulverize wheat and corn into flour and cornmeal in massive mills on both sides of the river. Ships docked in Richmond and loaded up with tobacco and flour, taking cargo all over the world and making fortunes for several families until the flow of money stopped.

The area's potential for windfalls from the Falls didn't go unnoticed by early English visitors. Gabriel Archer, on his 1607 trip up the James from Jamestown with John Smith and Christopher Newport, "estimated that one hundred English watermills could be powered by the Falls of the James." Before Richmond was Richmond, William Byrd II's land near the Falls was the colony's designated spot to build a warehouse along the river for tobacco inspection, starting in 1730. He also owned a gristmill on the south bank of the James in Rocky Ridge, today's Manchester, which he eventually sold. In 1733, when Byrd gave in to pressure from the colonial government to set aside land for a town where the Falls meet the tidal

James, he recognized that it was "naturally intended for marts where the traffic of the outer inhabitants must center."[26] And so it went, but it wasn't all smooth sailing.

Fits and Starts and Floods

In 1742, Richmond had 250 inhabitants, a mixture of merchants, enslaved people, fishermen and river men. When the colonial government declared in 1745 that Richmond would be a flour inspection site, it solidified the outpost's standing. To the north and west of Richmond, wheat became the predominant crop, and more corn, wheat and flour from the country headed to Richmond and to markets beyond.

In the mid-1700s, rudimentary mills, including Byrd's, utilized the river's rush to grind wheat into flour and corn into cornmeal and grits. Of course, one of the dangers of locating cities along the river was the uncontrollable nature of nature. In 1771, a flood tore through with forty-foot floodwaters, leaving a path of destruction.

Between floods and droughts, the river above Richmond often wasn't a reliable form of transport to town. When the river was low, heavy-laden craft couldn't make the trip. In early days of commercial river travel, boats unloaded at Westham, on the north bank of the river near the current Huguenot Bridge, and goods were carted down Cary Street, then known as Westham Plank Road, to get to mills and market in Richmond.

Wanting to take better advantage of Richmond's connection via the James to the Atlantic Ocean, in 1773 the government instructed the town to "build wharves and quays, to erect cranes and other things for the furtherance of the public good." Samuel Overton of Hanover County picked up a riverfront lot from William Byrd III's land lottery in 1772 and built a flour mill that added to the area's production capacity. Additional mills followed from the Oregon Hill area to Shockoe Slip.[27]

An international cast of characters financed the mills that turned Richmond into a milling monster. The Scotsman David Ross built his rudimentary mill on rocks in the river, and it was reached by traversing planks that connected rock to rock. Philip Haxall and his brothers left England, milling first on the Appomattox in Petersburg before purchasing the Columbia Mills in Richmond. Joseph Gallego, from Malaga, Spain, partnered with the Frenchman John Augustus Chevallie in business and in pleasure, as they married sisters from Philadelphia and purchased Ross's

Haxall Mills along the canal before the Civil War. *Library of Congress.*

mill. They expanded it many times over, moving eventually to Twelfth and Canal. And, of course, the enslaved Africans did most of the work, building, loading and unloading for no financial gain or notoriety.[28]

CANAL BUILDING

The next big thing to improve transportation and manufacturing involved building a canal to circumvent the Falls. George Washington and others hoped to connect the James to the Ohio River eventually so that Virginia could control trade from one end (at the time) of the country to the coast. Beginning in 1785, in fits and starts, with enslaved men and recent immigrants from Portugal, Ireland and Germany doing the dirty work of digging and hauling, the process took years. The James River Co. financed the first section from downtown to Westham, and by 1800, it was considerably easier to bring goods downriver from the west to Richmond, and the canal allowed boats to travel upriver on the canal. Equally important was that "the canal as it entered the city from the west could deliver a controlled flow of water from upstream and make it available to local manufacturers. There was so much drop between the upper level of the canal and the river below the falls that water drawn from the canal could be used to power one, two or even three."[29]

Engraving of canal, towpath and James River. *Library of Congress.*

Gallego Mills with a canalboat in front. *F.S. Lumpkin, Portrait and Landscape Photographers, Library of Congress.*

Once things got rolling on the river (and canal), in 1803 the James River Co. began charging tolls on the more than 170,000 bushels of wheat, 48,180 barrels of flour and 34,248 bushels of corn, among other items, that made the trek. Tobacco was Virginia's largest export, but flour was next. Virginia was the breadbasket of the young nation, and when the city was declared a customs district in 1800, everything unloaded and loaded was counted and taxed. Barrels marked "city flour" contained flour with superior texture and resistance to mildew to what the locals called "canal flour," since most of the inferior flour came from the country by canal.[30]

By 1835, Gallego stood as the world's largest mill, and still it grew. By 1848, it ground 5,500 bushels a day and its annual output was more than 120,000 barrels. Haxall Mills followed close behind in capacity. Just before the Civil War, the new twelve-story Gallego Mills building in Shockoe Slip (built by then-owners Warwick and Barksdale) used more than two million bricks to enclose 200,000 square feet with 293 windows and 29 doors.[31]

GOING GLOBAL

And where did all that flour go? To Africa, Europe, South America, Australia. By 1831, most of the 46,000 barrels of flour Gallego/Chevallie produced headed to South America. When the gold rush hit California in 1847, and masses of people needed flour to survive, most of it—743,000 barrels in the next ten years—came from Richmond's Gallego and Haxall Mills. That trip down the coast and around Cape Horn to San Francisco took four to five months.[32] Two factors determined why so much of the flour milled in Richmond wound up thousands of miles away. The mills of Richmond were noted for their blend of flour that held up well on months-long journeys below the equator. But some of the credit must go to the coopers who built the barrels that held the flour and kept it watertight. Water and heat can do wonderful things to flour, as a trip to Sub Rosa Bakery on Church Hill makes clear nowadays, but the combination in the hull of a ship on a nineteenth-century journey could spoil the goods.

Since so many ships from Richmond were offloading huge amounts of cargo in South America, primarily Brazil, it made sense to invest in something desirable for the return trip. Coffee and stones for ballast and bat guano for fertilizer and other goods made the trip back to Richmond. So much coffee came to Richmond on board these ships that for a time Richmond was the largest coffee marketplace on the East Coast.

ARAGON COFFEE
"Quality Sells It"—Always Uniform
ARAGON COFFEE CO., Inc.
Richmond, Va.

Left: Aragon coffee advertisement. The Aragon building is in Manchester on Seventh Street. *Special Collections and Archives, VCU Libraries.*

Below: The Haxall Flour Mills along the James River and Kanawha Canal with Gallego ruins sometime after April 4, 1865. *Library of Congress.*

Not surprisingly, coffee roasters and packagers built warehouses here, most notably the Aragon Coffee Roasters and the Cheek-Neal folks in Manchester, the latter part of the Maxwell House concern, and Antrim & Bowie in Richmond, which started in 1877 and eventually became what is now Old Mansion Foods in Petersburg.

Before the railroads altered the transportation system in Virginia, ships lined up to dock on both sides of the river. As an article from the *Richmond News Leader* recounts, "The center of the city's activity was the river dock, since it anchored vessels from all over the world: coffee from Brazil; sugar and molasses from the West Indies; salt from Liverpool, England; cloth from Manchester, England; herrings from Nova Scotia; lime from Maine; guano from Peru."[33]

In 1860, just before the Civil War brought exporting to a halt, 2,123 ships brought goods to the port and 2,337 headed out. That same year, the port of Richmond received 25,470 barrels of fish, 22,778 barrels of guano, 73,177 sacks of salt and 43,112 bushels of wheat. Ships sent on their way 423,194 barrels of flour and 143,000 bushels of wheat. Of those barrels of flour, 190,000 hailed from Gallego and 140,000 from Haxall Mills.[34] After the Civil War, with so much of the infrastructure burnt, including the huge Gallego complex, the flour milling industry never returned to its former glory. The Haxall and Gallego Mills were rebuilt, and Dunlop Mills reigned still in Manchester until the mid-twentieth century, but at diminished capacity. Both flour and coffee trades declined into the twentieth century, as larger ships couldn't easily make the trip to Richmond and the Hampton Roads area became the predominant port in Virginia.

Today, people crave biscuits and bread and pastries at several adorable local bakeries, and coffee roasters and baristas further their crafts in quaint coffee shops. Richmond is down to one city mill now, in the back of Sub Rosa Bakery on Church Hill, and one country mill, Byrd Mill, in Ashland. At Sub Rosa, brother and sister Evrim and Evin Dogu mill heirloom wheat and corn for the benefit of their wood-fired bakery patrons. James Beard Foundation semifinalists in 2017 as Outstanding Baker, they carry on traditions that harken back to Powhatan Indians grinding corn, Richmond millers grinding wheat and their own family baking bread and pastries with a Mediterranean sensibility. Right here in Richmond.

CHAPTER 4

THE BOUNTY OF THE JAMES

Sturgeon City

The James River that flows through Richmond was once known as the Powhatan, the King's River, and the king of the creatures within it was the Atlantic sturgeon, a fish with a prehistoric heritage. Sturgeon have roamed rivers and bays and oceans for more than 120 million years, and the bony plates, called scutes, along their spines help to pull off the prehistoric look.

Even just four hundred years of this fish tale is a whopper. The fish were so plentiful in the James in the 1600s that it was said one could walk across the river on their backs. Then in the 1800s, the demand for sturgeon roe led to so much overfishing that what had been a commonplace sight in Richmond became a rarity in the 1900s. Habitat loss and pollution further decimated the breed to a mere memory into the twentieth century. Catching sturgeon was banned in 1974, and it is illegal to possess one. Until 2004, researchers had no proof of a remnant sturgeon population in the river.[35] Now, every fall, it's possible to witness a five-foot-long sturgeon breach in the tidal James a few miles below the city, a sensational sign of the comeback of sturgeon to the river.

An anadromous fish, sturgeons lay eggs in fresh water but live much of the time in salt water until they journey back to their riverine birthplace to spawn. Atlantic sturgeon need a rocky bottom to lay eggs, and the area just east of the Falls of the James was once the perfect site. For centuries, the river and its tributaries teemed with sturgeon. William Byrd gave an account in his *Westover Manuscripts* of an Indian going to battle with what he called "those Royal fish":

A Virginia river full of fish. Perhaps a sturgeon is about to leap into the Indians' dugout canoe. *Theodor de Bry, engraver, and John White, artist, Library of Congress.*

In the Summer time tis no unusual thing for Sturgeons to Sleep on the Surface of the Water, and one of them having wander'd up into this Creek in the Spring, was floating in that drowsy condition....Soon as it came within his reach, he whip't a running Noose over his Jole. This waked the Sturgeon, which being Strong in its own Element darted immediately under Water and dragg'd the Indian after Him. The Man made it a Point of Honour to keep his Hold, which he did to the Apparent Danger of being drown'd. Sometimes both the Indian and the Fish disappear'd for a Quarter of a Minute, & then rose at some Distance from where they dived. At this rate they continued flouncing about, Sometimes above and sometimes under Water, for a considerable time, till at last the Hero Suffocated his Adversary, and haled his Body ashoar in Triumph.[36]

Since sturgeon can grow as long as fourteen feet and weigh hundreds of pounds, it's quite a feat of strength to wrestle one to shore. In 1705, Robert Beverly witnessed a similar lassoing and bucking bronco technique for bringing sturgeon to heel by the Powhatans. He remarked, "These sturgeons would also often leap into their canoes in crossing the river," which could be a reference to their mysterious breaching behavior that scientists are still studying.[37]

When John Smith and company explored the James in 1607, they saw the Indians pulling in nine-foot-long fish, and soon after, sturgeon became a crucial part of the colonists' diet. In his *General Histories*, he admits, "We had more sturgeon than could be devoured by dog and man, and which the industrious by drying and pounding, mingled with caviar, sorell and other wholesome hearbes, would make bread and good meate."[38]

Of course, the Native Americans caught the fish for their own use, but the colonists were looking for goods to export. Fishermen arrived from England to turn this surfeit of fish into a cash crop, but lack of salt and other preservation techniques doomed the plan. The few early sturgeon shipments to England didn't pass the smell (or taste) test.[39]

So the colonists kept the fish for themselves. William Byrd II included a "Receipt to Pickle Sturgeon & Make Caviar" in his writings (see chapter 24), and the fish remained a source of food in the colony, and eventually the new nation, but it wasn't considered a delicacy. Its abundance led Mary Randolph to include five recipes for sturgeon in her classic cookbook *The Virginia House-wife*. President Tyler was said to call sturgeon "Charles City Bacon," and others nicknamed it "James River Bacon" since it was such a mainstay for those living along the river. To the white and black men working on the river, sturgeon were a nuisance as much as a resource, tearing fishing nets with their bony scutes. It wasn't until the nineteenth century that there was a substantial commercial market for the roe and the James became the second-largest sturgeon fishery in the country.[40]

By September 25, 1856, the industry merited mention in the *Richmond Dispatch*:

> *Sturgeon Fishing is a profitable business. A fisherman who lives about twenty miles below Richmond, informed us, a few days since, that he was now catching from two to eight of these monsters with a drift seine every day, with the assistance of one person....Most of the sturgeon caught within thirty miles of this city are sent to our markets but not a few of them are salted and packed away for family use.*[41]

Looking down at the James River toward the east in 1865. *Anderson and Co., Library of Congress.*

Although they were not as appetizing as a sturgeon cutlet, other parts of the sturgeon were put to use and sold as well. The sturgeons' swim bladders were dried and processed to produce isinglass, a form of collagen that was used as a fining agent in brewing and winemaking to clarify the liquid. Isinglass also was used as glue for stamps and envelopes and even as gelatin in desserts such as blancmange. Fish heads were processed for their oil.[42]

The Civil War put a damper on the fishing industry on the James, but afterward, the market for sturgeon roe heated up. One cow (female) sturgeon could produce dozens of pounds of roe. By 1890, fishermen all along the East Coast caught 7.4 million pounds of Atlantic sturgeon, with about 700,000 pounds coming from Chesapeake tributaries, including the James. Much of the roe was shipped to Europe.[43]

In 1892, the writer Charles Washington Coleman witnessed a sturgeon meet its end:

And there, disposed in neat layers, is the roe—a million or more of the eggs, with all their life potentialities suddenly destroyed. It is this roe, of a glittering black hue, like shot of many sizes, that renders the cow sturgeon a so much more valuable catch than the buck. Occasionally two cows will yield a keg of roe, which is worth from eighteen to thirty dollars in the natural state. It is exported in large quantities to Germany and even to Russia…and much of it returns to our shores in the form of caviar.[44]

Ultimately, overfishing killed too many sturgeon and the commercial fishery itself. By 1920, the amount caught along the entire coast shrank to only 22,000 pounds. It wasn't long before Richmond newspapers bemoaned the state of sturgeon. In 1922, the *Richmond Times-Dispatch* reported that someone had caught an eight-foot, 250-pound sturgeon between the Mayo and Southern Railway bridges, the largest caught in the Fall Line in twenty-five years. What had once been not worth documenting was now news.

Water pollution and loss of habitat contributed further to the decrease in sturgeon sightings. The sturgeon population throughout the entire area was

Men on the banks of the James River and in boats fishing. *Special Collections and Archives, VCU Libraries.*

further decimated when, in the 1930s, one favored spot for spawning was dynamited for Richmond's deep-water port. Into the late twentieth century, many scientists thought there was little point to study the Atlantic sturgeon in the James, as there weren't enough there. In 2012, National Oceanic and Atmospheric Administration listed the Atlantic sturgeon as endangered, but with research biologists at Virginia Commonwealth University documenting sturgeon population and patterns, there's reason to believe that the sturgeon's story in the James isn't over.

SURGING STURGEON?

Now in the spring, shad and herring rush up the James River to where the tidal river meets the Falls in a frenzy matched only by the fisherfolks on the banks and in their boats. Best of luck to them, but the big catch around Richmond is the sight of a sturgeon. Scientists don't know why late summer is the time for sturgeon breaching or what it all means, but that doesn't lessen the spectacle of seeing a five-foot-long fish surge out of the water and leap into the air, several feet above the river, parallel to it for a moment, before returning to the depths with a satisfying splash.

Sturgeon wasn't the only fish worth catching in the river. Shad fishing in the James River, opposite Richmond. *From a sketch by W.L. Sheppard.* Harper's Weekly, *May 9, 1874. Special Collections and Archives, VCU Libraries.*

In September, it's possible to tour sturgeon stomping grounds with Discover the James on the James River Association's forty-foot pontoon boat. If you're as lucky as I was a couple of years ago, you'll witness a sturgeon breach in sight of William Byrd's Westover Plantation while hearing sturgeon stories and learning sturgeon science from Captain Mike Ostrander and VCU Rice Rivers Center biologist Matt Balazik.

Balazik has been studying sturgeon in the James for more than ten years, tagging as many fish as he can and receiving an e-mail every time a tagged sturgeon passes by designated markers in the river, bay and ocean. All that e-mailing leads to understanding sturgeon behavior so that researchers can determine what actions will improve their survival and spawning. There's a lot to learn on the two-and-a-half-hour boat ride. And a lot to look for. Everyone on the boat pays attention to Balazik's entertaining and educational commentary with one eye scanning the waterline, hoping for the thrilling sight of a sturgeon breaching. Passengers exclaim if they see it and moan if they miss it, eyes peeled for the next blast-off of the rocketing royal fish.

CHAPTER 5

BUCHANAN BARBECUES

Jasper Crouch and John Marshall

Some of the most memorable feasts of the late eighteenth and early nineteenth centuries in Richmond were concocted by a caterer and majordomo in demand, Jasper Crouch, a free black man, at the bucolic setting of Buchanan's Spring, just outside the city, where Hancock and West Broad Streets are now. The spot's simple pleasures included large oak trees to provide shade, an open-air shed with a large wooden table underneath for the ample meals and a clear stream flowing through the property, which had been inherited by a much esteemed Episcopal priest, the Reverend John Buchanan.

GETTING PUNCHY

The Richmond Light Infantry Blues, the second-oldest volunteer militia in the nation, founded in 1789, held festivities at Buchanan's Spring through the generosity of Buchanan, and they routinely enlisted Crouch to attend to their massive meals after parading and drilling. Crouch was a believer in pork heavily seasoned with cayenne pepper, among other specialties. Besides knowing his way around roasting a pig, Crouch distinguished himself further with his concoctions of punches and mint juleps that filled the massive, thirty-two-gallon India china punch bowl the Richmond Blues proudly set out at every celebration. His bartender chops gave the punch some serious punch.[45] And since a typical Richmond Blues July Fourth celebration at Buchanan Spring included dozens of toasts to the Revolution, to Washington, Lafayette and on and on, it's easy to imagine more than a few gentlemen punch-drunk by mid-meal. As the *Genius of Liberty* reported in 1826, the "Richmond L.I. Blues, with their guests, dined, as usual, at Buchanan Springs when the following toasts were drank with great hilarity and good feeling. The Spirit of '76—The electric flash, which purifies, while it enlightens." The toasts continued, so much so that the *Richmond Enquirer*'s sub headline, "Drunk at Buchanan Springs," makes perfect sense.

Crouch's prowess with the pig and the punch bowl caught the favor of another group of gentlemen who started their own social club in the late 1780s, including John Marshall, who later became chief justice of the United States and lived in Richmond throughout his thirty-four-year tenure on the court. The club's origins harken back to Scottish merchants in Richmond looking to gather a group of no more than twenty-five men for a simple meal every other Saturday from May until October under the auspices of the Amicable Society of Richmond. The original plan was simple enough, with "some cold meats for their repast, and to provide a due quantity of drinkables and enjoy relaxation in that way after the labors of the week." They limited expenses by initially outlawing wine and porter at their gatherings.[46] That didn't last long.

An engraving of Englishmen throwing quoits at megs. Visit the John Marshall House to give the chief justice's favorite game a try. *Virginia Cavalcade, Library of Virginia.*

By February 1801, the club had changed its name to the Buchanan Spring Quoit Club and made Buchanan its president, which made sense, since his hospitality allowed them their literal country club. With room to roam, they were better able to indulge in the popular game of quoits, a game brought over from England, similar to horseshoes. Two teams pitched quoits, circular rings made of brass or iron, onto (they hoped) stakes, called megs, in the ground. Marshall was a quoits aficionado, so he usually headed one team while the Reverend John D. Blair led the other. Games took place on both sides of the ample meal, and Crouch was the keeper of the rings, polishing the brass ones most members used and keeping Marshall's preferred heavy iron rings at the ready. Marshall was competitive enough that he was known to get down on his knees to measure the distance between quoits to determine the winning team.[47]

THE MEAL'S THE THING

Procuring the best ingredients to make a sumptuous meal was as competitive as the quoits. At each meeting, two members were assigned to act as caterer, which meant going to either Old Market on Main or New Market on what's now Marshall Street to buy the goods, staying within the club allotment. Here's just some of what $46.60 bought for a Quoit Club gathering in 1838: "A pig, 47 lbs of mutton, 15 lbs beef, 18 lbs sturgeon, 12 chickens, 2 large hams, 1.5 gallons brandy, 1.5 gallons rum, .5 whiskey, 12 bottles of porter and 1 pint of wine." Vegetables included potatoes, beets and cucumbers, and seasonings included cayenne pepper, mint and sugar. Lemon, eggs, butter, cheese and more rounded out the order.[48]

It was then up to Crouch to take the purchased goods and turn them into a celebratory and sumptuous meal. For his services, Crouch charged three dollars to butler and supervise the event, bringing his cart to take the supplies to the springs, providing ice and firewood there and paying cooks and servants.[49]

Watching the cooking was part of the entertainment of the day for the attendees. One visitor remarked that the roasting utilized the Indian method of cooking that John Smith had seen centuries before: a fire going underneath a platform made by four stakes with sticks across. Roasted pig was the main course of Quoit Club so often that the club's nickname was Barbecue Club. But there were many delights served at the table. One member recalled "deviled ham, highly seasoned with mustard, cayenne pepper, and a slight flavoring of Worcester sauce."[50] And years later, "Colonel Ellis wistfully recalled that he had never again eaten sturgeon cutlets to equal those prepared for the club."[51]

A RULING FROM THE CHIEF JUSTICE

A coveted invitation to the Buchanan Spring Quoit Club at 2:00 p.m., July 12, 1856, from Thomas Taylor to Henry Alexander Wise. *MSS 4 B8515, Virginia Historical Society.*

Quoit Club members included such luminaries as attorney John Wickham, who defended Aaron Burr in the trial of the century; president of the Bank of Virginia John Brockenbrough; physicians; military men; and merchants. The current governor of Virginia was an honorary member, and before each meeting, members called at the finer hotels to see if any worthy visitors might lend their wit to the event. General Winfield Scott was a regular attendee. In perhaps a stroke of genius, the rules included a prohibition on talking politics. The fine for flouting that rule was one basket of champagne brought to the meeting. On at least one occasion, Chief Justice Marshall ruled against the guilty parties, and the offenders produced the bubbly, though it had to be drunk from tumblers, as champagne glasses were not on site.[52]

It's likely that when John Marshall was the member in charge of the fête, he made sure some of his beloved Madeira made its way into Crouch's concoction for the quintessential Quoit Club Punch. An old recipe calls for "lemons, brandy, rum and madeira, poured into a bowl 1/3 full of ice (no water) and sweetened."[53]

Crouch's mint juleps were worthy as well. One visitor, Chester Harding, a portraitist in town to paint John Marshall, was invited to attend Quoit Club in 1826. As he tells it:

> *I watched for the coming of the old chief. He soon approached with his coat on his arm, and his hat in his hand, which he was using as a fan. He walked directly up to a large bowl of mint-julep, which had been prepared, and drank off a tumbler full of the liquid, smacked his lips, and then turned to the company, with a cheerful, "How are you, gentlemen?"[54]*

PRIORITIES

Crouch continued as a caterer and restaurateur until his death, when he was buried with full military honors by the Richmond Light Infantry Blues, such was their appreciation for his contributions to their celebrations over the decades.

It's possible to toast Crouch and this chapter in Richmond's history by taking a tumbler of barman Thomas Leggett's version of Quoit Club Punch at The Roosevelt on Church Hill. Or you can refer to his recipe in chapter 24, which is adapted from Dave Wondrich's recipe, which was adapted from the recipe above, which is as close as we'll ever get to the original.

The throwing of large metal rings after imbibing is optional.

CHAPTER 6

"CULINARY GENIUS"

Mary Randolph

As a Spanish immigrant, world-renowned chef José Andrés sees inspiration in a nearly two-hundred-year-old cookbook written by Richmonder Mary Randolph. Andrés, who became an American citizen in November 2013, says Randolph's cookbook reflects what the United States is about, and one of her recipes—for "gaspacha"—inspired the one served at his Tysons Corner American Eats Tavern, which closed in December 2016 and will move to Georgetown. "It will forever remind of where I came from and also where I now belong. Printed in her cookbook *The Virginia House-wife...*, it is proof of one of the earliest culinary influences my native Spain had on this country. Nothing defines America better than that book," he wrote in an online essay for *National Geographic*. "Her gazpacho recipe demonstrates just how far back the notion of this country as a cultural melting pot goes. Delicious and refreshing, it is just a small example of the many gifts that come from abroad."[55]

And in Mary Randolph's time, those gifts or recipes in her cookbook came from the enslaved women whom she oversaw in her kitchens, from the Native Americans who passed knowledge to early colonists and from her extended family's travels abroad. Along with gazpacho, Randolph included recipes for ropa veija, East Indian curry, West Indian gumbo and gougères—with cornmeal instead of flour—not to mention iconic southern fried chicken, the first recorded recipes for preparing black-eyed peas and hot sauce (a pepper vinegar). Plus, she included her own designs for a bathtub and refrigerator in her cookbook's second edition—that she says were stolen and then patented by a Yankee who stayed at her boardinghouse.[56]

Left: An 1807 portrait of Mary Randolph, a year before she opened her boardinghouse. *Library of Virginia.*

Below: Moldavia at Fifth and Main Streets, the former home of David and Mary Randolph. *Courtesy R.A. Lancaster, Library of Virginia.*

RICHMOND ROOTS

Mary "Molly" Randolph was born on August 9, 1762, on Ampthill Plantation in Chesterfield County, the eldest of thirteen children who then grew up on Tuckahoe Plantation in Goochland County. In 1780, she married her cousin David Meade Randolph, who was appointed a U.S. marshal, requiring a move to Richmond from their home on Presquile Plantation.

The Randolphs' downtown home, Moldavia—a blending of their two names by Edmund W. Rootes—became the epicenter of the Federalist social scene until Thomas Jefferson of the opposing Democratic-Republican Party became president and removed David from office. The loss of David's job compounded by a recession created by a fall in tobacco prices put the family on a downward financial spiral, necessitating the sale of Moldavia and a move to a rented house on Cary Street. And the Randolphs' bitterness toward Jefferson only grew.[57]

In 1807, when Aaron Burr was on trial for treason in Richmond, Burr's associate Harman Blennerhassett met Mary, whom he described as an accomplished lady of middle years but one with a biting tongue. She "ridiculed the experiment of a republic in this country" and "uttered more treason than my wife ever dreamed of." Never did he hear "more pungent" or better placed "strictures upon Jefferson's head."[58]

HOSPITALITY HOUSE

Both David and Mary struck out in new directions in 1808. Mary placed a newspaper ad announcing her new boardinghouse, and David became involved with the Black Heath Coal Mines in Midlothian.[59] According to writer Samuel Mordecai, "Mrs. R., who lacked neither energy nor industry, determined to open a boarding-house in 1808, feeling assured that those that had, in her prosperity, partaken of her hospitality, would second her exertions when in adversity."[60]

With her boardinghouse in what is now Shockoe Slip, and with another title given to her by Rootes, "Queen" Molly Randolph again would reign with her hospitality. "There were few more festive boards than the Queen's. Wit, humor and good fellowship prevailed, but excess rarely."[61] By 1810, the census listed Mary, not David, as the head of a Richmond household that included twelve slaves.[62]

AN AMERICAN ORIGINAL

Mary ran her boardinghouse until 1819, when she and her husband moved in with a son in Washington, D.C., and she began work on *The Virginia House-wife*, the first cookbook that truly explored the bounty of Virginia and included an entire section on its vegetables.

"Nothing in the history of early American cookbooks quite prepares us for the sumptuous cuisine presented by Mary Randolph," writes culinary historian Karen Hess. "She brought her personal flair to everything she did,

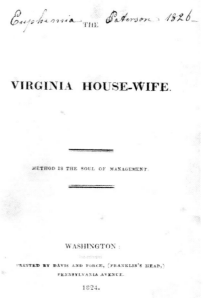

Above: The 1810 census shows Mary Randolph as head of household with twelve slaves. *1810 U.S. Census.*

Right: The 1824 title page of the first edition of Mary Randolph's *Virginia House-wife, Method Is the Soul of Management. Elizabeth Robins Pennell Collection, Library of Congress.*

but her reputation as the best cook in Virginia and the early success of her work indicate that her cookery was solidly based on Virginia produce and practice. Perhaps the most remarkable aspect of her cookery is its eclecticism, which flowed from the fascinating interplay of strikingly different influences that manifested themselves from the very beginning."[63]

While Mary was penning recipes for families who had access to the plantation larder and a separate building where cooking was performed by the enslaved, she also provided tips on frugality and time management, with the mindset that "the government of a family bears a Lilliputian resemblance to the government of a Nation."[64]

Mary knew it was vital that those running the kitchen learned the best ways to use and preserve all parts of an animal. "Mrs. Randolph gave clear, explicit directions for curing beef, ham, bacon and herring and for making souse, black pudding and sauces, and for pickling sturgeon. She took no short cuts."[65]

Despite despising Thomas Jefferson—whose daughter was married to her younger brother—Mary had no trouble incorporating into her book some of the products Jefferson introduced to Virginia, such as the vanilla bean and macaroni. She even sent him a first-edition copy and received a reply, which is in the National Archives' Founding Fathers Papers project:

Monticello Mar. 30. 25.

Th Jefferson returns his thanks to mrs Randolph for the valuable little volume she has been so kind as to send him. it is one of those which contribute most to the innocent enjoyments of mankind, and which give us the useful instruct on how to employ to our greatest gratification the means we may possess, great or small, a greater degree of merit few classes of books can claim. with his thanks he prays her to accept the assurance of his high respect and esteem.

ILLUSTRIOUS INFLUENCES

After Mary's book came out in 1824, her youngest son, Burwell, was involved in a crippling accident on a ship, and she spent the rest of her years nursing him in D.C. She died in 1828, before the third edition of her cookbook was released, and was buried in what would eventually become Arlington Cemetery.

The Virginia House-wife influenced many black and white cooks who followed, including the first African American cookbook writer, Malinda Russell. "I cook after the plan of *The Virginia House-wife*," says Russell in her self-published 1866 book, and in turn, she also recognizes from whom she learned—Fanny Steward, a black cook from Lynchburg.[66]

Mary, much like the cooks in her kitchens, was pretty much forgotten about until 1929, when her grave was found. However, it wasn't until 1970, when a facsimile of her cookbook was published, that historians took another look.

James Beard, the dean of American cooking, touted Mary Randolph three years before his death in 1985. In a 1982 *Richmond News Leader* article, he called her a "far-seeing culinary genius" because she encouraged readers to use tomatoes in seventeen different recipes when people still thought the fruit was filled with poisons. "At a time when few people thought about tomatoes at all, she provided food recipes for tomato ketchup, tomato marmalade and tomato soy," Beard wrote.[67]

Yep, tomato soy. We're leaving it up to you to try that recipe.

CHAPTER 7

A RED FROM SORROW

Daniel Norton

I n late 2013, we headed into the basement of the Virginia Museum of Fine Arts. We were ushered into a climate-controlled art warehouse of sorts—painting after painting hung on panels that you could flip through as you would rugs at HomeGoods. We were at the end of a mini quest: we wanted to see the portrait of the Richmond man who had cultivated a hybrid grape on a farm in what is now the Carver District near Virginia Commonwealth University.

Writer and friend Todd Kliman had recently released his part history, part memoir, *The Wild Vine: A Forgotten Grape and the Untold Story of American Wine*—a riveting tale about his own and vintner Jenni McCloud's obsession with Dr. Daniel Norton and his grape, but it contained no image of him.

Norton's circa 1815 portrait—painted about the time he graduated from medical school—is owned by the Ambler family, which his mother married into in 1799 after Norton's father died. However, while the painting is in possession of the Virginia Museum of Fine Arts (VMFA), the family retains usage rights.[68]

Eyeing the crazed canvas up close in the VMFA's underground storage area, we saw a young man of about twenty-one years peering back with closed lips, sporting long, dark mutton chops, a black topcoat and yellow waistcoat—a man who had not yet experienced crippling heartache.

By his mid-twenties, Norton was living at his twenty-seven-acre Magnolia Farm with his wife, Elizabeth Call, whom he married in 1818. Three years later, he lost her and their first baby during labor.[69]

Above: The Friends of Shockoe Hill Cemetery with the Norton portrait at the Virginia Museum of Fine Arts in early 2017. *Judy Smith Photography.*

Left: "The Norton Grape." *Fleischman, 1867. Special Collections, USDA National Agricultural Library.*

GRIEF GROWS

While grieving, Norton traveled to New York and returned with a renewed interest in viticulture. He turned to his gardens at Magnolia Farm, which were just outside city limits, near Buchanan's Spring and near Columbia, the home of the Philip and Clara Walker Haxall at Lombardy and Grace Streets. Mrs. Haxall herself was a noted gardener, having "beautiful trees, shrubs and flowers" and serving five different nuts to guests—all grown on her land.[70]

Norton kept copious notes and diagrams on what he planted and where. Sometime around 1821, he cultivated a new vine, the Norton, which Mrs. Haxall supposedly named, from a seed of one of his Bland vines and open pollination from other vines nearby.[71]

His grape, "Norton's Virginia," was included in the 1867 book *The Grape Culturist: A Treatise on the Cultivation of the Native Grape* by Brooklyn's Andrew Fuller:

> *It seldom ripens so as to be eatable in this vicinity, and is too harsh and sour to make wine. Farther south, and in some parts of the West, it is said to become sweet, at least sufficiently so to make an excellent wine. It is quite hardy, and remarkably free from disease. The vineyardists of Hermann, Missouri, esteem it as one of the best and most reliable wine grapes they have. Bunches very long, occasionally shouldered, not very compact. Berries small, round. Skin thick, black. Flesh a little pulpy, rather harsh in flavor. A strong healthy grower. Leaves pale bright green. Ripens here middle to last of October.*[72]

A Norton wine produced by Stone Hill Winery in Hermann received a commendation at the 1873 Universal Exhibition in Vienna, with critic Henry Vizetelly saying that Norton from Missouri would one day rival the great wines of Europe. Stone Hill Winery won the first of eight World's Fair gold medals in Vienna, and by the turn of the century, it was the second-largest winery in the country.[73]

FROM OBLIVION TO ACCOLADES

But soon, Norton, who died of dysentery in January 1842, and his grape, except in rarified horticulture circles, was virtually shelved. Dry laws in the

South and national Prohibition in 1920 prompted the neglect and mass destruction of vineyards in Virginia and Missouri, where the grape thrived.[74]

Here's where Virginia winemaker McCloud comes into the picture. She was at the 1995 American Society for Enology and Viticulture conference when she first heard of the Norton grape and fell under its spell.[75]

Through McCloud's search and subsequent plantings at Chrysalis Vineyards in Middleburg; a 2004 history that Clifford and Rebecca Ambers researched for the *American Wine Society Journal*; Kliman's detailed book; and the Friends of Shockoe Hill Cemetery,* where Norton is buried, his story lives on, through deed and drink.

Cheers to Norton, "the Real American Grape," as trademarked by McCloud, who, during an April 2017 interview, said she believes she now has the world's largest planting of Norton grapes—some forty acres.

*In May 2017, a monument marking the 175th anniversary of Norton's death was installed at Shockoe Hill Cemetery. McCloud helped with the monument's funding.

CHAPTER 8

WOMEN REVOLT

1863 Bread Riot

C ivil War stories are a Richmond staple, and it's not surprising that there are noteworthy food-related tales, though, in one case, it was the lack of food that was notable. At the start of the war, the city's population was 38,000, including 14,275 slaves and free blacks.[76] As many parts of Virginia became battlegrounds, displaced Confederate citizens and sympathizers fled to the relative safety of Richmond. Also converging on the new capital city were government workers, military men and speculators, increasing the population dramatically to more than 100,000 by 1863. They all needed to eat. It helped that farms surrounding the city could provide much of what was needed. As the war dragged on though, more women handled the farming with so many men gone fighting, which only added to their work.[77]

As it became clear that the war wouldn't be over quickly, hospitals were established by the Confederates, including what became the largest in the world, Chimborazo, on Church Hill. A mini-municipality with gardens, pastures, goats and cattle, a dairy, a bakery and five icehouses, it supplied the thousands of sick and wounded who lingered there. Tobacco factories were turned into soup kitchens to feed prisoners and wounded soldiers.[78]

Spying Opportunities

Those living in Richmond still loyal to the Union found ways to use food to help their cause. Elizabeth Van Lew, a Richmonder who lived on Church

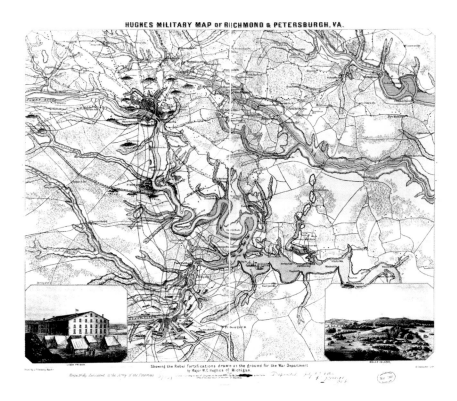

An 1864 map of the Richmond area. Note Libby Prison. *Hughes military map of Richmond & Petersburgh (sic), Va. drawn on the ground for the War Department by Major W.C. Hughes of Michigan, 1864. Library of Congress.*

Hill with her widowed mother, became a spymaster for the Union bit by bit, plying Confederate commandant David Todd with ginger cakes and buttermilk to get him to acquiesce to letting her visit wounded Union officers in hospitals. Unbeknownst to him, she used a custard dish with a secret compartment to pass messages back and forth when she visited. Van Lew relied on her slaves (though she was opposed to slavery—a contradiction hard for us to understand) to do much of the delivering of messages and food. She had hot rolls delivered to the Henrico jail just down the hill to Union officers under threat of death and brought "chicken soup and cornmeal gruel" to prisoners from Bull Run.[79]

The kitchen played an unexpected part in the famous Libby Prison break in 1864, as it was the enormous kitchen chimney that provided cover for the officers digging the tunnel to freedom outside the notorious prison.

After many weeks of work, 109 officers escaped overnight, humiliating the Confederates as about half of the Northern men made it to Union lines to tell the tale.

FOOD FIGHT

These days in Richmond, thousands of hungry Richmonders often hit the streets for a food festival or the latest beer release. But back in 1863, the women who gathered in Capitol Square on April 2 were deadly serious... and very hungry.

After years of war and deprivation, the middle class and working women, some of whom were left to struggle on their own by male relatives who had fought and, in some cases, died, were desperate for food. The farms outside town produced less each year with so many men away at war. The Union blockade made trade via the river more difficult. Prices were out of control. By April 1863, flour was $200 a barrel. Sugar rose to $20 per pound and bacon to $8 a pound, and chickens sold for $6 each. According to the March 29, 1863 *Richmond Daily Examiner*, "The city bakers sold loaves in three sizes at $1, $2 and $3 a piece. These were ridiculed as being so slight that, according to one cynic, the middle loaf almost required a microscope to see and the smallest certainly did."

The Confederacy had stores of meat, flour, potatoes and coffee to provide for its troops, and soldiers were legally allowed to confiscate food from the markets at much lower prices than the public paid. That led some producers to hold back their stores from the army, awaiting better prices, and also to hoarding among many who had the means. Reports of stolen food in Richmond during the war became increasingly common. Newspapers reported robberies of $500 in groceries, 625 pounds of bacon, barrels of flour and 77 pounds of sugar. It's likely the plunder found its way to the wartime black market.[80]

The spring of 1863 produced a series of unfortunate events that made life especially hard to take in the city. An explosion on March 13 on Brown's Island at a small munitions factory killed sixty-nine, mostly girls and women. A snowstorm dumped nine to twelve inches of snow in the city on March 19–21, and when the snow melted, the roads were in horrific shape, which made transporting food into town almost impossible. To add insult to injury, the city waterworks failed right after the storm so that many had to go to Capitol Square or the river for water rather than more conveniently located hydrants.[81] And preposterously, on March 27, Jefferson Davis called for a day of fasting and praying for all Confederates, which did not go over well with those already feeling famished.

Bread or Blood

On April 1, a group of women gathered at Belvidere Baptist Church on Oregon Hill to come up with a plan. They decided to demand food from the governor the next day or take it by force. Mary Jackson, a woman who worked at the New Market, one of the leaders of the group, hoped to get the governor to agree that they should be able to buy food at the same prices as the military.[82]

The next morning, dozens of working-class women from Oregon and Sheep's Hill in the west and Rockett's and elsewhere to the east converged at Capitol Square at the George Washington equestrian statue with whatever weapons they could scrounge up: axes, hatchets, knives, clubs and, in one case, an empty pistol. A smaller party went to the Executive Mansion to request a meeting with Governor John Letcher but was turned away, as he was already at work in the capitol. When he did come out to address them at the statue, they demanded "bread or blood." He was unmoved, so the women moved out of the square down Ninth Street toward Cary Street, weapons at the ready. It was eerily quiet. The crowd grew, and some boys and men joined them as they continued into the business districts of Cary and Main Streets, grabbing carts and wagons along the way.

Reportedly, the first offender was "a toothless, old woman" who used an axe to break the door of a Shockoe Slip warehouse and made off with five hundred pounds of bacon with the help of some young men.[83] Another widow took $100 worth. One grocer pulled out a revolver to defend his store on Cary. A confectioner begged the crowd to take his goods without wreaking havoc. The crowds split and smashed windows and went after more than food in some cases, looting shoes, clothing and other goods.

Soon the mayor of Richmond, Joseph Mayo, arrived and read the riot act, to absolutely no effect. For two hours, groups took what they could, breaking into multiple stores, a government commissary and warehouses on Cary, Main and Franklin Streets, from Twelfth to Eighteenth Streets. One woman was about to commandeer a wagonload of beef until the driver, a man she knew, told her it was destined for smallpox patients at a city hospital. She relented, but some others took it from him and drove off with the beef. At

Frank Leslie's Illustrated Bread Riot, 1863. *Library of Congress.*

some point, Jefferson Davis begged the crowd to stop and promised them what bread he had, but it did not appease the crowd.[84]

The governor called out the public guard and confronted the rioters on Main Street. Letcher stood on a cart and threatened to have the guard shoot into the crowd if the mob didn't disperse within five minutes, looking at a watch as the men readied their weapons. His threat worked, and the crowd disappeared with no shots fired.[85]

Hundreds, if not more than a thousand, people took part in what was known as either the Bread Riot or the Holy Thursday Riot. Most got away unpunished. Approximately forty-one women and twenty-four men were arrested, including one fairly well-to-do woman who owned 127 acres in New Kent County. Margaret Pomfrey had come to town especially for the protest and felt she had to do her part for those in need. Most of those arrested weren't convicted. Martha Fergusson, who was found with two barrels of flour, several hams and a barrel with traces of butter from one of the looted shops, received only a ten-dollar fine and a day in jail.[86]

Though the Confederate government tried to suppress the news, reports of the riot made it into the Northern papers, which embarrassed the Confederacy. Most Southern writers tried to spin that true Southern women did not take part in the riot, but rather, as the *Richmond Examiner* reported, "a handful of prostitutes, professional thieves, Irish and Yankee hags, gallows-birds from all lands but our own."

In a last twist, Governor Letcher pardoned most of the convicted offenders because the city jail was overcrowded—and he didn't have food to feed them.

CHAPTER 9

LIFE LESSONS FROM BEHIND THE BAR

John Dabney and Wendell Phillips Dabney

D uring Reconstruction in Richmond, famed caterer and bartender John Dabney—an African American business owner with prominent white clients and owner of a three-story Broad Street house in the middle of a white neighborhood—told his middle son, Wendell, "All of your books haven't taught you never to let a white man know how much you really do know about anything except hard work."[87]

While admired by white Richmonders, Dabney encouraged his children to be cautious of whites, to be entrepreneurial and to own property, which his wife, Elizabeth, did prior to the end of the Civil War and then leveraged to the couple's advantage.

Two of the Dabneys' children, Kate and Hattie Eva, became Richmond teachers. Another son, Milton Williamson, became a well-known baseball player and postal employee. Wendell, also a talented musician and composer, attended Oberlin College for a year, taught in Louisa County, founded two Cincinnati newspapers that crusaded for black rights and served as the first president of Cincinnati's NAACP chapter.[88]

It was Wendell, born seven months after the fall of Richmond in the Civil War, who spent the most time behind the bar working with his father, John, often accompanying him to summer catering gigs at places such as Little Red Sweet Springs and Alleghany Springs. "Being John Dabney's son and an attaché of the bar was an open sesame one way or the other everywhere. Smiles and glad hand came galore. I learned to mix drinks and I strove unsuccessfully to imitate Pop in the fine art of the profession." It was John, often hot tempered and known for carrying a gun to work, who helped to shape Wendell's world and political views.[89]

John, who finished paying for his own freedom two years after the Civil War ended, was immortalized for that act in the poem "Little Jack" by Hanover County's Thomas Nelson Page and then mentioned again by Page in a November 1904 *Scribner's* magazine piece as an "old time negro," beholden to his female owner out of "deep and abiding affection"—a notion that *Richmond Planet* newspaper editor John Mitchell described as "touchingly pathetic" in an editorial a month later.[90]

HANOVER TO HOTELS

It was Wendell who corrected Page and other writers' accounts about his father's payments in the *Richmond Planet* in May 1938.[91] Born into slavery in Hanover Junction in 1824, John was owned by Cora Williamson DeJarnette. As a teenager, he first traveled as a jockey for Cora's brother William Williamson and then found work as a waiter in Gordonsville.[92] By 1850, according to a city directory, William had moved to Richmond to manage the St. Charles Hotel (also known as City Hotel), and John came too, learning to cook under William's supervision. During this period, John was working under the self-hire system, in which the enslaved worked for employers, sharing a portion of their wages with their owners. He also was able to make tips. Masterful at public relations, he often sent bowls of his famous terrapin stew and mint juleps to the *Richmond Whig*'s editorial department, no doubt looking for good ink and getting it.[93]

By 1860, John was working at the Ballard House, a hotel in Richmond, connected by an iron bridge to the Exchange Hotel on East Franklin Street. These hotels catered to those attending slave auctions in Shockoe Bottom and also held auctions in their basements.[94]

About four years later, John was able to purchase the freedom of his wife, Elizabeth, whom he married by 1856, for $1,400 from Arthur Morson, who had threatened to sell her. She and John had just had their first child, Clarence, and she apparently was diverting some of her attention away from Morson's family. At the time, John was making payments on his own freedom to Cora DeJarnette but asked her if he could delay them and use that money instead to secure his wife's freedom.[95]

Right: Portrait of John Dabney. *The Valentine.*

Below: The Ballard Hotel at Fourteenth and Franklin Streets, April 1865, connected by a bridge to the Exchange Hotel. *Library of Virginia.*

PAID IN FULL

Toward the end of the war, some intriguing land deals involved John's wife. In July 1864, Elizabeth, then a free woman, and Virginia A. Taylor were given a lot on Leigh Street between Adams and Brook Avenues from Thomas L. Courtney, a railroad company clerk. Elizabeth immediately purchased Virginia's share of the lot and then resold it and an adjacent lot John owned in August 1866 for $5,000 to the Richmond Railway Company. By 1895, Elizabeth's benefactor, Thomas L. Courtney, was superintendent of the Richmond Fredericksburg and Potomac Railroad Company.[96]

In November 1866, according to Wendell's memoirs, John accidentally nodded at an auction he was walking by and made the winning $4,950 bid on an eleven-room home on Broad Street between College and Jail Streets, near his family's church, First African Baptist—a home that he stipulated for the sole use of his wife, "free of all of his or future contracts." John also completed his outstanding freedom payments to his former owner by 1868, earning him widespread respect and, most importantly, good credit throughout Richmond.[97]

CONTESTS AND CATERING

John also competed in mixologist contests across the state and those that brought in bartenders from outside Virginia. In an accounting of one contest by his son, "the one who came from the famous St. Charles Hotel of New Orleans was the most formidable contender for Julepine honors. A mistake in regard to the time sent Pop's sublime effort into the hall three hours ahead of the appointed moment, but it won, hands down." For one winning effort, the City of Richmond awarded John a fourteen-inch-tall silver quart cup with six silver straws that was engraved with "John Dabney, presented by the citizens of Richmond for champion juleps."[98]

By 1869, according to city directories, Dabney ran a restaurant at 806 Main Street, near the Spotswood Hotel, which survived the burning of downtown Richmond in April 1865 but succumbed to fire in December 1870. He then ran a restaurant at the end of the Richmond and Petersburg Railroad line at 803 Byrd Street by 1871.[99]

"No man ever made a better [diamond-back] terrapin stew than John Dabney," said a chef from New York's Delmonico's who visited Richmond. "In the years that followed, amidst the race prejudice which gave white

John Dabney's restaurant at 806 Main Street, circa 1869, near the Spotswood Hotel at Eighth and Main Streets. *Library of Congress.*

caterers the preferences, John Dabney always made the terrapin stew, Virginia's most costly dish," Wendell wrote. The elder Dabney also was known for his canvasback duck, oyster preparations, venison and Mongolian pheasant, and he catered for Richmond's corporate elite, which included Lewis Ginter and Peter Mayo.[100]

John fell ill and died at his Broad Street home on June 7, 1900, and his son Milton was left to cater a huge railroad gathering in a Petersburg warehouse that day.[101]

The day after he died, the *Richmond Times-Dispatch* wrote, "For many years he had charge of nearly all the best barbecues in the state....He had the reputation of being the best man living to mix mint juleps....He was one of the best known caterers in the South."[102]

HONORING DABNEY

In November 2015 at the Quirk Hotel, Richmond's first dinner to honor its most famous African American caterer and bartender was held during Fire, Flour & Fork. Attendees included a descendant and food and drink historians. At the second dinner in 2016, Jennifer Hardy, the great-great-granddaughter of John Dabney, attended with her family members. John Dabney's daughter Kate married Baxter Jackson, and they had a son, Dr. Julien Dabney Jackson Sr., who was Jennifer Hardy's grandfather.

Jennifer, who retired from teaching in Brooklyn in June 2017, moved to Kentucky, where she once galloped racehorses, as John Dabney did when he was a teenager. Her son, Jeremy, is a musician, and her daughter, Elsa, is a foodie. "It's nice to know where these genes originated," she said. As for John's engraved silver cup with the six silver straws, John's son "John" Milton Williamson Dabney was last photographed with the cup, and he died in November 1967. He reportedly was to give the cup to his son, John "Jack" Milton Dabney, with whom he lived in Newark, New Jersey. Jack, who ran a funeral home, died in 1987 in Newark. He was married to Fannie S. Clay Robinson, who had been married for twenty years to movie star and tap dancer Bill "Bojangles" Robinson, also of Richmond. The couple had no children, and the search for that cup continues.[103]

But there is one silver-plated item that you can see that was owned by John Dabney and given to Kate Dabney Jackson—an egg boiler that John purchased in 1870 when the city was auctioning off the contents of the White House of the Confederacy, which was being converted into a public school for white children and was near his Broad Street house. Kate donated the egg boiler back to the White House of the Confederacy after it reopened as a museum. The piece is now part of the collection at the American Civil War Center. Kate and her sister, Hattie Eva Dabney Gray, are buried at Evergreen Cemetery.

CHAPTER 10

HOMEMADE SUCCESS

Pin Money Pickles and Suffrage

You know you've made it big when a bank in your hometown uses your success story to woo customers, implying that they may make it as big as you did with your Pin Money Pickle recipe.

That's exactly what American National Bank did in November 1919.

By that time, Ellen G. Tompkins Kidd was running a pickle processing plant at 1500 West Marshall Street that produced one thousand barrels a day—a long way from mixing up batches of the family's recipe for gherkins at home and selling them to make a little extra "pin" money.[104]

In 1868, sixteen-year-old Ellen was making pickles in her parents' home from her great-grandmother's recipe, selling them to friends and winning prizes at the state fair. Four years later, she still was selling her pickles from the basement of her 619 North Sixth Street home with the encouragement of her lawyer husband, John Boulware Kidd, when an order came in from Seattle, Washington, for five barrels (or 150 gallons of pickles). She thought it was a mistake and sent the customer five gallons. She received a telegram: "Barrels, barrels, five. Could eat five gallons by myself."[105]

Kidd traveled to Chicago in 1873 to visit a friend, and during that trip, she met two men from the Pullman Company, Major Dangerfield and Captain Angel, who changed the course of her business. "I remembered them because of the angel and the danger. I think I took them by surprise, because I was younger then, and very much dressed up, and when they refused to see the samples which I had carried along, I plead that I had never been on a Pullman car, and that I should like to go on one. Well, they couldn't very

Above: A 1920 ad from the *Virginia Cookery* cookbook produced by the Virginia League of Women Voters. *Susan Winiecki.*

Left: Pin Money Pickle factory at 1500 Marshall Street. *The Valentine.*

well refuse me that. When we went into the diner, they let me taste some of their pickles, which were in a delightful state of fermentation, but of course I said nothing about that. After I had somehow eaten the pickle, I said, 'Now I've tried yours, won't you try mine?' Well, of course they couldn't very well refuse me that, either." By the time Kidd returned to Richmond, she had an $800 order for Pullman passenger railway dining cars, which in turn exposed her product throughout the country.[106]

In a Pickle

That Pullman order and others meant literally getting herself out of a pickle when it came to her supply chain, so Kidd reached out to family member William Taliaferro in Essex County to help her grow enough burr gherkins (a wild cucumber originally from the West Indies) to meet increasing demand. He organized farmers in Essex and four surrounding counties to plant acres of gherkins. When the cucumbers were ready for harvest, he set up pickle-brining stations in strategic locations so that ripe pickles could be preserved on their way to Richmond.[107]

In 1898, her family—Ellen and John had four children together—moved to 706 East Leigh Street, where her pickle "kitchen"/plant was built in back of her house. By 1910, she had moved her "kitchen" to a new five-

Portrait of Ellen Kidd. *From* Virginia: Rebirth of the Old Dominion.

Pin Money Pickles were on the menu of the St. Charles Hotel as well as the Jefferson in Richmond and the Plaza in New York. *New York Public Library.*

story plant on Marshall Street. Kidd, a masterful marketer, took out a half-page ad in the March 20 *Times-Dispatch* to tell her own story, which included a drawing of her Leigh Street house and "kitchen" with the headline: "The Phenomenal Growth of an Unusual Enterprise." She included a customer fan letter and a coupon for a free sample jar. Pin Money Pickles also were appearing in hotels across America and in Europe—from the Plaza in New York City to the Hotel Chamberlin in Virginia—each hotel bound to use the trademarked name on its menu. They were even served at the White House.[108]

"The public likes the homemade product," Kidd said, "and you can maintain the homemade standards in the factory as well as in the home."[109]

Her supportive husband passed away in 1910, and she sold her Leigh Street house and moved into the Shenandoah apartments on Allen Avenue—one of her many real estate investments. She incorporated as Mrs. E.G. Kidd, Inc., and her company became a Richmond Chamber of Commerce member in the fall of 1913.

WOMEN'S WORK

In 1909, a small group of Richmond women formed the Equal Suffrage League of Virginia. Attending rallies in Capitol Square and elsewhere, Kidd and the league worked to obtain the women's vote until three-fourths of the state legislatures (but not Virginia's) ratified the Nineteenth Amendment in 1920. The suffrage league then disbanded and formed the Virginia League of Women Voters, of which she was a charter member and treasurer.[110]

By 1927, she had sold her controlling interest in the company, retiring to the Shenandoah. The company continued production in Richmond until 1950.[111]

A suffrage rally on the steps of the Virginia Capitol, May 1, 1915. *The Valentine*.

Kidd, who died in 1932, was the only female member of the Richmond Chamber of Commerce for years, and she also served on the board of Sheltering Arms Hospital for more than twenty years.[112]

Of her early zeal for promoting her product, both in person and through the mail, Kidd said, "I think I must have been the original woman drummer." Only she used pickles as her drumsticks.[113]

CHAPTER 11

EXTRACT AND IMPACT

C.F. Sauer Company

A particularly pleasant multisensory experience in Richmond can be had by heading west on Broad Street, watching for the twenty- by sixty-foot vanilla sign atop a brick building before turning onto Hermitage Road. Make sure the car windows are rolled down to catch a whiff of the aromatic entities in the hopper at The C.F. Sauer Company. The scent could be cumin or cinnamon or a mix that hints of Thanksgiving. Whether or not the iconic incandescently lighted rectangle atop the Richmond-born-and-bred company is twinkling like the eyes of the burly baker, within the bowels of the brick buildings, home to the spice manufacturer since 1911, stacks of sacks of pepper await grinding, vanilla extract lingers in enormous vats and one of Richmond's oldest and proudest businesses keeps a multitude of flavors flowing. Since the plant is rarely open to the public, those lucky enough to get a tour of its inner workings can attest that it's a cross between an unusually fragrant multilevel maze and Willy Wonka's factory.

Founded by Conrad Frederick Sauer, known as Cuno, in 1887, The C.F. Sauer Company, which celebrated its 130th anniversary in 2017, is a family-run enterprise, manufacturing flavoring extracts, spices, herbs and other tasty products. Cuno was born in 1866 in Richmond to his German immigrant father, Conrad, and his mother, Sarah, the daughter of German immigrants. In an autobiographical sketch from 1918, he remembered moving to Germany with his parents for a few years when he was nine years old, a foretaste of the international travel he would do later in life to grow his business into a behemoth.[114]

These women at C.F. Sauer Company are sorting nutmeg. Some will stay whole and others will be ground. *The C.F. Sauer Company Archives.*

At age thirteen, young Sauer worked as a store cashier. A customer cheated him out of four dollars, which, he later remembered, "served to sharpen my wits on the money question." By age eighteen, he worked in Richmond as a drug clerk for Boedeker Brothers, learning the retail and wholesale drug business.[115]

When his father died and left him an inheritance, he figured it was time to open his own store, which he did on his twenty-first birthday in 1887 at Seventeenth and Broad Streets. At first, he ran a traditional drugstore of the day, "doing a general jobbing business, such as cigars, cigarettes and groceries." He eventually distinguished his shop from others since he had noticed that housewives often came into drugstores to refill their own bottles with flavoring extracts and other products. So he began producing vanilla and lemon extracts in five- and ten-gram small bottles at consumer-friendly prices, displaying them in branded cartons with the Sauer name and logo and promise of purity prominent in the company's advertising. Shoppers were smitten by the convenience and price, and since the company delivered the goods by horse and buggy to other shops and grocers around the city, sales grew quickly.[116]

EXHIBITING EXCELLENCE

In 1889, Sauer married Olga Hassel, also born in Richmond to German immigrants, and she went right to work alongside him, coming to the plant in the evenings to stir and test the vanilla and other extracts while he caught up on paperwork. Her not-so-little exhibit at the 1889 State Fair of Virginia won first prize and set the stage for the company's carefully choreographed participation in trade shows and expositions in Atlanta, Baltimore, Chicago, San Francisco, Paris, Antwerp, Buenos Aires, Rome, Madrid and London, where Sauer's flavoring extracts won gold medal after gold medal, all the while dazzling consumers and retailers with elegantly furnished booths and high-quality products. Closer to home at the Jamestown Exposition in 1907, their extract received a silver medal. Sauer Sr. was concerned enough to write the jury secretary, only to be assured that the silver was the highest honor awarded for extracts at that event.[117]

By 1909, Sauer products were sold in twenty-seven states and were even getting shipped to Europe by special request. Sauer concentrated more fully on the extract business and ramped up production of extracts to include rum, sherry, almond and even Old Virginia Fruitti-Punch extract, to a total of thirty-two flavors. The company's growth necessitated a few moves around downtown until settling at its current location at 2000 West Broad in 1911, then a state-of-the-art showplace for manufacturing extracts. In 1927, a Richmonder eating a memorable dish at a Tokyo restaurant wondered what the secret ingredient was and was flabbergasted when told it was Sauer's vanilla, all the way from his hometown.[118]

One employee said C.F. Sauer Sr. insisted on procuring raw goods by the trainload. He wasn't kidding. *The Valentine.*

A longtime employee, Lula Pugh, who started in 1914 and eventually became the extract forewoman, remembered filling bottles one at a time with a rubber tube. That has changed, but the cold-pressed method for making vanilla extract that the Sauers perfected in the 1880s is still employed today, albeit on a much larger scale. Another longtime worker recalled in 1957 that if Sauer Sr. couldn't buy the raw goods by the trainload, he wasn't interested. He needed top-quality raw goods on hand in huge quantities to fill the millions of bottles his glass factory, another acquisition, turned out. By its twenty-fifth anniversary in 1912, C.F. Sauer had become the largest producer of extracts in the United States. Only then did Olga start to take a salary: fifteen dollars a week.[119]

Expansion

The 1920s saw the addition of spices to the company repertoire. Cuno had always wanted to add a mayonnaise to the line but hadn't found a recipe that met his standards. After Sauer Sr.'s death, in 1927, C.F. Jr. became president and became acquainted with Mrs. Eugenia Duke's brand of mayonnaise, headquartered in Greenville, South Carolina. She'd made a name for herself and her mayonnaise making sandwiches for soldiers stationed nearby during World War I and eventually bottled and sold the mayo. Sauer Jr. bought Duke Products in 1929, and the rest is tomato, mayonnaise and white bread sandwich history. It was an important acquisition for the company, as Duke's has a fanatically loyal and growing customer base but also because C.F. Sauer III married a daughter of one of Duke's salesmen.[120]

Sauer's moved away from metal spice containers when it became the first company to use and manufacture plastic spice containers, holding the patent for it. The company has expanded its product lines over the decades and now has a footprint well beyond Richmond, including its The Spice Hunter line in California and, of course, Duke's in South Carolina, which just celebrated its 100th anniversary. More than 750 people work in the various brands of the company, from coast to coast.

The headquarters, along with extract and spice production, remains in Richmond with the fourth generation of the Sauer family at the helm, with members of the fifth generation working there as well, continuing the family tradition. When asked what the secret is to be successful for 130 years in business, Conrad Sauer IV, president of the company, says it's his family's relationship with its employees: "Generations of Sauer leadership have

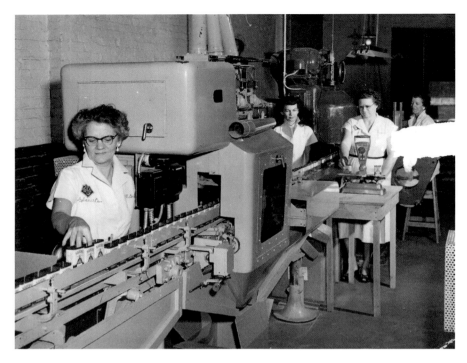

A long line of women work the pepper line at Sauer's. *The C.F. Sauer Company Archives.*

treated employees like family and have given them full responsibility to do their job and trusted them to do it."

Over the centuries, tastes have changed, and the market for once beloved Old Virginia Fruitti-Punch extract is no longer, but cinnamon, black pepper and many other products retain their place in the C.F. Sauer pantheon. And bakers everywhere keep adding pure vanilla extract to the batter.

Olga Sauer said of her husband, Cuno, in a seventy-fifth anniversary commemorative article in the *Greenville News*, "He was determined to have his product pure. If it couldn't be pure, and the best, he wasn't going to do it."[121] Cuno Sauer's innovation and inclination look (smell and taste) like pure genius.

CHAPTER 12

THE MEAT JUICE OF THE MATTER

Valentine's Meat-Juice

Necessity truly was the mother of invention for Mann S. Valentine II in 1870. His wife, Ann Maria Gray Valentine, mother of their seven sons, lay ill upstairs in their home on North Second Street, wasting away. She had been sick for weeks, and her doctors were unable to do anything more. Her husband decided to take matters into his own hands—and basement. With his wife losing strength, unable to keep any food or medicine down, he relied on his one year of studying chemistry at the College of William and Mary and worked in his cellar on a process to make a potion by "extracting pure juice from meat, concentrate it and preserve it without losing any of its strength-giving properties" in hopes that she could recover. On New Year's Eve 1870, he succeeded. As she improved noticeably and steadily, his family, neighbors and doctor friends were so amazed that they wanted to try the product themselves. With his dry goods retail experience on tap, his entrepreneurial spirit took hold, and he turned his basement into a business. Valentine's Meat-Juice changed the family fortunes in more ways than one.[122]

THE MEDICINE GOES DOWN...AND AROUND

To our ears, meat juice sounds nauseating, the opposite of its purpose, but an 1892 medical text, the *N.Y. Medical Times*, volume 19, notes Wyeth's beef juice, Bush's Bovinine, Murdock's Liquid Food and Armour's extract

Mann S. Valentine II, the inventor of Valentine's Meat-Juice and benefactor of the Valentine. *The Valentine.*

of beef, not to mention Mosquera Beef Cocoa and Beef Jelly. Valentine's product was "a clarified aqueous extract of lean beef." His two-ounce bottles contained the concentrated juice of four pounds of lean beef. The recommended dose was one teaspoon diluted in three tablespoons of cold or warm water two or three times a day. That distinctive egg-shaped bottle would need a refill pretty quickly at that rate. "Whenever the stomach from irritability fails to retain either food or medicines, the Meat-Juice may be employed to prepare that organ for their reception."[123]

Valentine wasted no time patenting his preparation and, by December 1871, had patents in Great Britain, France, Isle of Man, Ireland, Belgium and, of course, the United States. He opened a manufacturing spot at Tenth and Cary Streets and began advertising in Virginia newspapers that year, marketing "The Germ of Life." The concoction soon won awards, including a gold medal at the Virginia State Agricultural Society in 1871, the International Exhibition in Philadelphia in 1876 and the Paris Universal Exhibition in 1878, as well as others, for purity and efficiency. The juice had a dark red wine color and was slightly syrupy, hence the instructions to dilute it in water.[124]

Valentine worked with physicians to improve and test the product and welcomed their testimonials. Dozens of physicians extolled the wonders of it in helping patients recover from yellow fever, seasickness, pulmonary tuberculosis, influenza and many other afflictions. As the marketing materials said, it was the "Food par excellence for a Tired Stomach." More than one doctor credited it with curing him and/or a member of his family. A doctor in Providence, Rhode Island, wrote, "Valentine's Meat-Juice was the only nourishment retained by my five-year-old daughter during an attack of Pneumonia. I consider that it saved her life."[125]

The company was deft at getting the product out and about, including using family connections in the tobacco business to cultivate sales to Britain. Valentine sent the bottles with missionaries bound for China and

Japan, which spread the Meat-Juice gospel as well. It certainly was a coup when King George V's personal physician, Emperor Yoshita of Japan, the Empress of Russia and China's great viceroy all gave written testimonials of how it helped their recoveries from serious illness.

IN THE PRESS

Admiring stories appeared in papers across the country. "Not only is the Meat Juice used in case of sickness, but as an article of food in compact form, as a Summer drink instead of liquor, and a beverage at the table of the wealthy, it has grown into great popularity....In travelling, persons who are liable to suffer from changes of water are simply foolish to be without it. To the consumptive, especially where distressing thirst, nausea and faintness are symptoms, it is the greatest boon ever conferred." National newspapers reported in 1881 that President James Garfield, after being shot, was served toast and Valentine's Meat-Juice.[126]

Not everything in the paper proved good news for the company. Two instances of people using bottles of Meat-Juice to try to hide arsenic poisoning occurred in the Seddon and Maybrick criminal cases in England.

The infamous egg-shaped Valentine's Meat-Juice bottle from an advertisement. *Valentine Meat-Juice Records, The Valentine.*

The news improved in 1900 when the British Supreme Court of Judicature ruled in the favor of the U.S. company against the Valentine Extract Company operating in England using the Valentine name. Once the imposter company paid its fine, it manufactured Valtine's Meat Globules. Honest.[127]

In the early days, the story went that every time Valentine received a large order, he'd head to the bank to get a loan to purchase the cattle he needed to produce the elixir in large amounts. The company expanded and moved several times, building an impressive headquarters at Sixth and Cary Streets. From a young age, his sons worked in the company, and when he died in 1892, eldest son Granville Gray Valentine became president, a post he held for fifty-one years. The elder Valentine's will included an estate valued at $275,000. A bequest of $50,000,

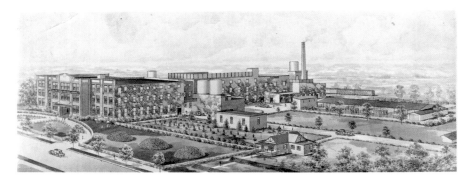

The sprawling Meat-Juice plant at 1600 Chamberlayne Avenue—an example of farm to bottle. *Valentine Meat-Juice Records, The Valentine.*

Valentine's collection of archaeological artifacts and the family home on East Clay Street established the first museum in Richmond, the Valentine, Richmond's history museum. Some of the family focused on the museum, while others worked in the family business.

Soon after Valentine's death, another tragedy struck when the headquarters on Cary Street went up in flames. The company rebuilt promptly and kept growing. In 1895, as Valentine's continued to expand production, it purchased forty-six acres in what then was the country at 1600 Chamberlayne Avenue and moved its abattoir from Twenty-Fifth Street and Nine Mile Road to the new site. Cattle arrived at the new location by railcar and fed on fields of hay, alfalfa and corn before it was time to be butchered.

The plant was a marvel of meat, and as the juice production left a lot of solids, side businesses flourished so that not one bit was wasted. Employees, both black and white Richmonders, usually ate pretty well, taking meat home, but hearts, livers, tongues and entrails were sold to butchers. Both shin bones and tibias could be turned into knife handles, and the horns and hooves were sold to button manufacturers. "The head bones go to sugar refineries for use in clarifying sugar; hides to tanners, tripe are sold to sea coast towns for bait." Dried beef residue was ground for animal and poultry food.[128]

MODERN MEAT

In 1906, the secretary of agriculture visited the plant and pronounced it "eminently clean, light, airy and sanitary in every respect, and have no criticism to make of this establishment." He did not ask the cattle for their opinion. When the company outgrew its headquarters downtown in 1920, it moved its entire operation to a modern facility on Chamberlayne, where its abattoir had moved years before.

By 1925, the original product was for sale in Hong Kong, Bombay, Ceylon, South Africa, Australia, Europe, Mexico City and beyond. It had been taken on expeditions to the North and South Poles and the African jungle. No wonder Valentine's manufactured as many as 600,000 bottles of Meat-Juice a year. There was no limit to its usefulness, according to its own pamphlets: "The time for using the Meat-Juice, besides during illness,—Just before or after meals; on rising in the morning with a feeling of debility; or, on retiring at night and not disposed to sleep"; "A very pleasant and inviting Jelly may be made….Chicken broth will be improved"; and my favorite, "In the administration of the Meat-Juice by enema, the directions are the same as when taken by the stomach, except that the quantity should be larger." Indeed.

Valentine's Meat-Juice was said to be the not-so-secret ingredient in the Bloody Marys at the Commonwealth Club, the exclusive men's-only spot on Franklin Street where the Valentines were members. Other products were added to the company's lineup in the 1920s and '30s, but none ever approached the popularity of the Meat-Juice. Alas, the company ceased production decades ago.

The Valentine Museum has, among its many treasures, one of the finest costume collections in the country, the stunning Neoclassical Valentine-Wickham house and much of Mann II's brother Edward V. Valentine's sculpture collection. And of course, there's the display of Valentine's Meat-Juice that started the whole enterprise all those years ago. There's been talk of a rebirth of the product. It could work in tandem with Richmond's distillery, brewery and cidery craze, for as Mann Valentine V said, "Valentine Meat Juice over ice is just the thing for hangovers."[129]

CHAPTER 13

CULTIVATING TASTE

From T.W. Wood to Ellwood's

Richmond restaurant chalkboards and menus often pay tribute to the farmers and purveyors who deliver ingredients to the kitchen door that are integral to the dishes proffered that same day. At the annual Elby awards, the dining community's celebration put on by *Richmond* magazine, farmers get a category to themselves, an acknowledgement of their contributions to the dining community. The farmer's work starts with a seed and a story.

Timothy Ward Wood, son of a farmer and seedsman in England, immigrated to the United States after his father died, arriving in post–Civil War Richmond. Initially, he started farming outside town. The war had decimated the South's seed supply, and getting seeds from the North proved difficult. In 1879, Wood started selling seeds out of his home. He soon struck deals with ship captains in Richmond for free shipping of seed from England since his bulk orders acted as ballast on the ships. Soon thereafter, he set up shop downtown as T.W. Wood & Sons.[130]

PRODUCING PRODUCE

Through the catalogue it began producing in 1883, the company touted offerings for crop growers raising animals: "Field peas make the best ham." For farmers raising vegetables and fruits for market, Wood's marketing of Brooks' Nutmeg Cantaloupe seeds, procured from Mr. Brooks of

Gloucester, Virginia, was a coup: "This is the first year Mr. Brooks has parted with any seed, and what we have secured is from his finest melons."[131]

Wood and his sons certainly learned the ways of Virginia. One grandson remembered that they'd drive Civil War veteran farmers, in town to place orders, out to battlefields that surrounded Richmond and listen "to them relate their vivid recollections, while enjoying a sip or two of 'The Receepee,' usually made with Wood's grains. This kindness would generally be rewarded with a larger seed or implement order."[132]

In 1897, the U.S. Department of Agriculture purchased more than $10,000 worth of seeds from Wood & Sons under the heading of Purchase and Distribution of Valuable Seeds. The establishment sold hundreds of varieties of seeds, including Wood's Extra Early Hanover Cantaloupe, Cow Peas and Pamunky Ensilage Corn. By 1900, Wood & Sons was the largest seed house in the South, having won a gold medal at the 1900 Paris Exposition, followed by the grand prize in 1904 in St. Louis, Missouri.

T.W. died in 1905 at age sixty-five, widely known and admired. He had been president of Richmond Grain & Cotton Exchange as well as the American Seed Trade Association.[133] His sons Henry and William continued the business, which eventually included seed farms and trial grounds in Chesterfield, Caroline and Amelia Counties. The company's warehouses were located at Fourteenth Street next to Mayo's Bridge and then at Eighteenth and Franklin. The office and store stood at Fourteenth near Main with branch stores near the market at Sixth and Marshall and the Seventeenth Street market as well. One employee says he used roller skates to fill orders in the sprawling warehouse.[134]

Wood's Brimmer tomato took home the gold medal in 1907 at the Jamestown Exposition, where its display featured "seeds in beautiful giant crafted glass cylinders." Presentation may not have been everything, but the beauty of their seed catalogues, which by 1893 were in color, and other promotional materials cannot be overstated. The bounty of Virginia on display in colorful prints along with helpful advice and detailed instructions certainly enticed customers to ogle the offerings. Both the Library of Virginia and the Valentine have collections of these beauties. T.W. Wood & Sons ceased operations in 1956, but several decades later, another venture would dig into the past.

Seeds and Stories

Southern Exposure Seed Exchange (SESE) in Louisa County has taken the seed business back to the basics, saving seeds from heirloom vegetables and cultivating almost forgotten varieties that have been elbowed out by hybrids to keep the flavors of years gone by close at hand. Among its more than 130 varieties of tomato seeds is the Radiator Charlie's Mortgage Lifter Tomato, a story in a seed. Whether canning, slicing or just trying to relive a taste from childhood, you'll find the tomato of your dreams here. If you have a hankering for a German Red Strawberry Tomato or a Richmond Green Apple Cucumber, SESE has the seeds and the cultivating know-how to help you keep taste alive. Its stock, more than 70 percent organic, includes the Brimmer tomato that won the gold medal at the Jamestown Exposition in 1907 for Wood & Sons.

Ira Wallace, an early advocate of seed saving and evangelist for heirloom varieties, helped in 1999 bring SESE to the ACORN intentional community in Louisa, where it has thrived since. Its colorful catalogues are works of art and science and offer gardeners of all levels knowledge and power and a connection to the Southeast's agrarian past. The Southern Foodways Alliance awarded Wallace the Craig Claiborne Lifetime Achievement Award in 2016 for her work with SESE, telling the stories of seeds so people keep planting for flavor and beauty.[135]

From Seed to Soil

The Pendergraphs, Jo and Rob, turn heirloom seeds into produce for restaurants and consumers. They started Manakintowne Specialty Growers at Monacan farm in eastern Powhatan in 1985. As Jo tells it, "We grew an herb and vegetable garden with our friends next to a horse barn, where we had access to good sun and well-composted manure." At first their garden was for their own pleasure, but soon they realized chefs would be interested in what they were producing—fresh herbs and vegetables that weren't otherwise available locally. Their flavorful seasonal salad mix—a mix of mustard greens, sorrel, radicchio, arugula, pea shoots and blanched peas—was quite the upgrade from romaine or iceberg and was an immediate hit. It's still what they're best known for. They bought the current farm property, also in Powhatan County, in 1988, eventually building a house and moving there in 1997. They added greenhouses, high tunnels and ten acres, so now they produce herbs, tomatoes, salad greens and more on twenty-one acres that had previously been a hayfield and cow pasture.

While Manakintowne isn't certified organic, they've improved the soil by adding organic matter, crop rotation and cover crops. Pendergraph notes, "Although we have not been through an organic certification process, we use only natural fertilizers and OMRI-approved organic botanically derived pesticides, and we use them sparingly, as we build our soil organically. Wildlife habitat, pollinators and vegetative buffers are important components of the farm."

Pendergraph's husband, Rob, originally walked into restaurants with product lists and samples. Once the couple sold to chefs including Rob Hamlin at DuJour, J Frank at the Berkeley Hotel, Greg McDaniel at Lemaire, Paul Elbling at La Petite France, Michelle Williams at the Island Grill and Jimmy Sneed at the Frog and the Redneck, among many others, word of mouth did the sleight of hand and made the produce disappear.

Amy Hicks of Amy's Organic Garden didn't expect to become an organic grower even though her grandparents in Harrisonburg had an "enormous garden" and her grandmother canned all kinds of garden produce. Hicks wasn't planning on a farming career; she managed a Richmond restaurant. Her husband, George Ferguson, introduced her to organic vegetable gardening. In the 1990s, they had a large home garden, "growing all kinds of interesting varieties you just didn't see in the grocery stores at the time. One day, Manakintowne Growers dropped off a product list at the restaurant where I worked, and I thought, 'Hey, this is all the stuff we are growing!' and the idea of growing for a living set in. Manakintowne was a big inspiration for us then and still is!"

They first sold their goods out of their backyard garden not far from Forest Hill Park (where the South of the James market is now). Basil was the first product they sold, to Chez Foushee and Mainly Pasta. Ellwood Thompson's and farmers' market sales followed. In 1998, they moved to three acres in New Kent County, and when they outgrew that, they made the move to Charles City County in 2004. That land had been conventionally planted, so it took three years building the soil with cover crops to become USDA certified organic in 2007, one of the few certified organic farms in central Virginia. Hicks is a friendly and knowledgeable presence at the markets in Richmond and Williamsburg, encouraging people to eat with the seasons and take what nature gives. The farm's almost one hundred Community Supported Agriculture (CSA) members give the business a reliable income in the growing season, and Cherokee Purple tomatoes, colorful peppers and unusual varieties of vegetables, not to mention Amy's beautiful flowers, keep the throngs coming to her booth at the South of the James and Birdhouse markets in Richmond, as well as the Williamsburg Farmers Market.

TO MARKET, TO MARKET

Donnie McCaffery moved to Richmond in 1985, after owning a natural foods store in New Orleans, to open Good Foods Grocery in the Stony Point Shopping Center. He attributes some of the growth in the healthy food scene here to Michael King of the gone but not forgotten Grace Place, an all-vegetarian restaurant downtown from 1973 to 1996. Good Foods has doubled in size over the decades, and the fact that the store stocks 350 jars of herbs and spices and 450 bins of bulk food "speaks to how beautiful food is and with a great message—less packaging." With Ellwood Thompson's and others, McCaffery said, "We all started a revolution, and it really took off."

Ellwood Thompson's wasn't started by a guy with that name but by two guys named Rick Hood and Eric Walters. They opened City Market in 1989

Ellwood Thompson's aims for a one-hundred-mile radius for getting local fruit and vegetables. *Ellwood Thompson's.*

to offer organic and natural items to customers in a three-thousand-square-foot spot and, in 1993, moved to Carytown into a former A&P. Over the years, now solely owned by Hood, ET's has grown to meet customer demand and taken over much of the shopping center. Its twenty thousand square feet includes a juice bar, natural products, butcher and seafood sections, as well as a bakery and prepared foods. As farming around Richmond has made a comeback, ET's was an early adopter of the local food scene. More than two dozen farmers within one hundred miles of the store provide produce, dairy and meat and poultry to Ellwood's. To celebrate that connection, Amy Hicks of Amy's Organic is the focus of an exuberant portrait in its Beet Café.

In 2015, Hood and McCaffery were among the founders of Real Local RVA, a nonprofit, collaborative effort among farmers, local independent grocers, restaurants, makers and purveyors to better connect the disparate components of the local food system. It's all about growing relationships and businesses together and making it easier for consumers to find healthy, local food where they shop and eat.

CHAPTER 14

LEWIS GINTER'S LARDER

The Jefferson Hotel

By the time Lewis Ginter conceived of building his grand hotel, the Jefferson, for his beloved adopted hometown of Richmond, he had crossed the Atlantic thirty times and stayed at countless fine hotels on his around-the-world travels. At his townhome on West Franklin Street, he had on at least one occasion entertained five hundred people, bringing in a renowned chef from New York City to cater the elaborate affair.[136] After a career that included building a tobacco company (Allen & Ginter), a townhome considered one of the finest homes in the South (on West Franklin), a suburb (Ginter Park) and a country estate (Westbrook), among other efforts with more to come, he focused his millions and his design sense on giving Richmond a significant piece of architecture. In that, he shared something with his hero and the namesake of the hotel, Thomas Jefferson, who had a century before seen to it that the Virginia Capitol would give architectural gravitas to the new capital.

GRANDEUR REIGNS

Ginter tasked designers to incorporate the best features of his favorite resorts into his luxury hotel. After fits and starts with another firm, he called on Carrère & Hastings to deliver the impressive edifice. When the Italianate- and Spanish Renaissance–style hotel opened on October 31, 1895, Richmonders were in awe of its appointments and amenities, which

The interior of the Jefferson Hotel before the 1901 fire. *Cook Collection, The Valentine.*

included a rooftop garden, two toilets on every floor, men's and ladies' billiard rooms and electric lights. Immediately thereafter, out-of-towners staying there for the wedding of artist Charles Dana Gibson to Richmond society gal Irene Langhorne, soon to be immortalized as the Gibson Girl, were impressed as well.[137]

The ladies' entrance on Franklin Street led to Ladies' Parlors (where Lemaire is today) and a Ladies' Café off the Palm Court where the Edward V. Valentine statue of Thomas Jefferson stood (and still stands) in all his Carrara marble glory. The men's entrance was off Main Street, and both the Grill and the Smoking Room were nearby and paneled in a manly aesthetic. The former had a "'tilting oyster-kettle' and an icebox from which patrons chose their steaks." Barman John Barber presided over a thousand-bottle wine closet. If that wasn't enough, he could send someone through a trapdoor to the even more extensive holdings in the wine cellar.[138]

The luxurious dining room on the mezzanine level above (where the Empire Room is now) could seat three hundred diners, and its rococo carpet was as ornate as the ceiling. Monsieur Durand was the French chef who oversaw the one kitchen that produced the dishes available on the extensive menus.[139] Up to date and enormous, it boasted "a huge mechanical refrigerator, a dish warmer, a whole department for cakes, pies, and puddings, a giant steam table, a dishwasher, a butcher shop, a fifteen-foot pastry range, and ice cream freezers."[140]

FARM TO MENU

Suggestions for exploring Richmond on a marketing piece for the Jefferson Hotel. *New York Public Library.*

And it was all quite necessary. The second general manager of the hotel, P.M. Fry, was in constant correspondence to acquire the best of everything from squab and other wild game from a Philadelphia purveyor, who could ship the pigeons at $3.25 per dozen by express, and a Beaufort, North Carolina enterprise that could supply eggs at 21 cents a dozen. In March 1905, Drohan & Co. in New York apprised the hotel staff that "we will ship you fresh killed chickens and broilers and small stuff, but turkeys will be frozen as this year's supply of fresh turkeys is about over." J.B. Dickinson was eager to ship daily to meet the hotel's needs: "The soft shell crab season is sufficiently advanced to enable us in furnishing you nice prime crabs, that is, nothing less than 4½ inches in length. We beg to advise you that we will make you daily shipments, or as often as you desire, of 10 dozen or more for $1.40 a dozen."[141]

Vegetables were grown for the hotel restaurants at Jefferson Gardens, just north of Ginter's summer estate, Westbrook. The stock farm he invested in, Bloomingdale Stock Farm, was a large dairy four miles north of the hotel with more than one hundred head of choice dairy cattle, Jerseys and Holsteins, that produced butter and cream for the venture.[142] The hotel proudly offered some of Richmond's own products, including tobacco, of course; Pin Money Pickles; and its own Jefferson brand of Aragon Coffee, the Jefferson Straight Mocha and Java Coffee. Several varieties of Virginia oysters were a standard offering.

The Jefferson as it looked from the Franklin Street side around the time of the 1901 fire. *William Henry Jackson, Detroit Publishing Co., Library of Congress.*

The hotel survived Lewis Ginter's death in 1897 and a catastrophic fire in 1901, but it took several Richmond investors, including Joseph Bryan and Major James Dooley, to bring it back to full Beaux Arts beauty in 1907. It remained a place of grand entertainments and lavish meals, hosting presidents, entertainers and national heroes until it lost its luster mid-century. Unfortunately, segregation was in full force in Richmond, so though many hotel employees were black, black guests were not welcome well into the twentieth century. One occasional employee in the dining room was purportedly Bill "Bojangles" Robinson, the performer, who in his early days waited tables in between touring. During the Beaux Arts Ball in 1933, Robinson, by then a well-known actor and dancer, performed in the Rotunda but was not allowed at the hotel as a guest.[143]

Richmond native Bill "Bojangles" Robinson performed at the Jefferson in 1933 but was not allowed to stay there due to Jim Crow laws. *Carl Van Vechten, 1932, Special Collections and Archives, VCU Libraries.*

Later, private clubs, including the men's-only Rotunda Club, took over large sections of the hotel, keeping the statue of Thomas Jefferson from public view from 1949 to 1977 and taxing the kitchen with their extravagant buffets.

By 1980, the hotel had closed, and talk commenced of knocking it down to build a new Federal Reserve Building on the site. Thankfully, another group of investors, spearheaded by George Ross, saved the hotel from destruction. Oddly enough, one of the most famous meals ever served at the Jefferson was during this limbo period. In December 1980, *My Dinner with Andre* was filmed in the ballroom of the then-shuttered and unheated hotel. Directed by Louis Malle, the acclaimed film was written by and starred Wallace Shawn and Andre Gregory. The majority of the 111-minute film consists of the two friends conversing intensely over dinner in a set made to look like the Café des Artistes in Manhattan.

THE RENAISSANCE IS REAL

In 1986, when the Jefferson Hotel finally reopened as the Jefferson Sheraton Hotel after six years of being closed, its new restaurant, Lemaire, which was placed where the private Rotunda Club had been and before that the Ladies' Parlor, won high marks out of the gate. *Washington Post* restaurant critics Phyllis Richman and Carole Sugarman wrote, "Two extraordinary lobbies, with marble and gilt in luscious excess are anterooms to Lemaire restaurant—named after Jefferson's personal maitre d'hotel—which is a labyrinth of handsome rooms." They note the menu had contemporary and traditional elements: "duck with hazelnut oil and ginger (the best of the dishes I tried). On the traditional side are Virginia peanut soup and a fine, fresh crab and corn chowder. The staff, dressed in morning coats, serve with hushed formality; the food is presented with high style."[144]

Walter Bundy, who led the kitchen at Lemaire as executive chef from 2001 to 2015, placed a renewed emphasis on using excellent local products. In a 2002 History Is Hot dinner at the James Beard House in New York, he included Manakintowne Specialty Growers' frisée lettuce on the menu. Sean Brock, now a James Beard award–winning chef and author based in South Carolina, worked for Bundy as his sous chef for two years. When Lemaire closed for several months in 2009 for a complete renovation, Bundy oversaw the transformation of the menu, designed to appeal to a broader audience. *Esquire* immediately approved, naming it one of the Best New Restaurants of 2009. Richmond embraced the tangerine lounge area and the new approach, as well as the terrace when it opened a few years later. The dining rooms are as lovely as ever, named, fittingly, Gibson, Ginter, Valentine, the Library and the Conservatory. A trial of honeybees on the roof and an herb and vegetable garden outside the hotel were additions that surely would have made Ginter nod in approval.

Lemaire isn't the only option for getting the flavor of the place. Afternoon tea is a lovely option for multiple generations, and holiday visits to view the elaborate gingerbread concoctions of the pastry chefs enchant all ages. The extravagant weekend brunch or a beer and a bite at the warm and casual TJ's make it easy to add a touch of tradition to today.

In 2017, after another extensive renovation throughout the hotel, the Jefferson once again received Five Diamond and Lemaire received Four Diamond status from AAA. Patrick Willis, executive chef at Lemaire since 2016, continues the tradition of incorporating Virginia's finest ingredients into the menu. In 1900, one marketing piece said of the Jefferson, "A meal here will always leave a fragrant recollection." At the time, the aroma might have been from smoke wafting upward from the Smoking Room to the Dining Room. But for many years at Ginter's grand hotel, it's been the sweet smell of success.

CHAPTER 15

IN THE DRINK

Prohibition and Pop

On November 1, 1916, more than three years ahead of the rest of the nation, Virginia went dry. A mere thirty-three years after Richmond counted 163 saloons within its boundaries, in a capital city where politicians toddled over from the Capitol to the Executive Mansion to partake from a five-gallon bowl of toddy in days of yore, the Mapp Law, outlawing the manufacture or sale of alcohol in Virginia, was the law. It didn't matter that Richmond, Petersburg, Alexandria and Norfolk had voted to stay wet in a 1914 referendum. The Anti-Saloon League and Woman's Christian Temperance Union had turned the tide; by 1909, eighty-six of one hundred Virginia counties had no saloons.[145]

Just three hundred years before, as noted in *Every Home a Distillery*:

> *Colonists had little choice about whether to drink alcohol. Non-fermented drinks did not yet exist, and they had no way to prevent the juice of apples, pears, plums and other fruits from fermenting. Tea remained an expensive luxury item until the second half of the 18th century and coffee was unavailable to most colonists until the late 18th century.*[146]

Many Virginians had made arrangements before the ban went into effect by stocking up at home. There was also a little leeway for obtaining a cure for what ailed you. For decades, physicians kept brandy and whiskey at the ready, and pharmacies, including the earliest version of

Owens & Minor, dispensed whiskey for medicinal use. "Every ten days, patients willing to pay about $3 for a prescription and another $3 or $4 to have it filled could get a pint of booze."[147]

CHOOSE OR LOSE

Brewers had a choice of their own: close down or switch to producing soft drinks. Suddenly, advertisements for cola, ginger ale and lemon and strawberry and sarsaparilla filled the newspapers: Christo Cola, Chero-cola, Oka-cola and many more bottled away downtown. Home Brewing, which had been brewing beer since the late nineteenth century, made the transition by purchasing Beaufont Lithia Company in Chesterfield County. Beaufont had been selling the spring water that flowed over granite on its property, which gave it a pleasant minerality, and making ginger ale as well since the late 1800s. In 1912, it boasted that it was the largest bottler of ginger ale south of New York. The actual spring was in Chesterfield County, near the Boulders office development, where the spring house still stands.

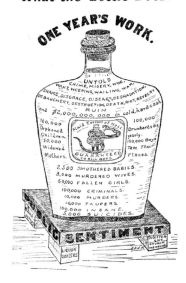

What the Bottle Does.

The temperance movement had statistics and emotion on their side… for a while. *Special Collections and Archives, VCU.*

Oddly enough, Beaufont had a little trouble with the law itself. The U.S. Department of Agriculture issued a judgment against Beaufont Lithia for misbranding its product in 1911. The report noted ginger and capsicum in the ginger ale but "that there was nothing used in the manufacture of the product which would entitle it to be termed 'the perfection of purity and excellence,' nor the 'highest quality,' nor medicinal." Ouch. Plus, two bottles were only 75 percent full. The fine was $650 plus court costs. The brand recovered its dignity enough to be served at the Jefferson Hotel in the 1920s.

Home Brewing developed another product near the end of Prohibition: Climax Ginger Ale. Since it wasn't alcohol, they had to make it sexy somehow! It was known in Richmond as much for

Above: The Thirteenth Annual Convention of the Anti-Saloon League of Virginia at the Virginia Capitol, January 21, 1914. *Thomas Sparrow, photographer, Library of Congress.*

Left: Home Brewing Company on West Clay Street in Richmond transformed into a soda maker in 1916 to survive the Mapp Law and later federal Prohibition. *Maureen Egan.*

its twinkling sign that beckoned to motorists driving at night on the old Lee Bridge as for its highly acidic flavor. The bottle said "Pale Dry." The flavor said gut busting.

Of course, soda wasn't quenching everyone's thirst for eighteen years. Franklin County might have been the hotbed of distilling and bootlegging during Prohibition, but the counties surrounding Richmond put up a good fight. Thousands of stills were destroyed in Powhatan and Chesterfield Counties, and Henrico wasn't far behind. In Richmond, more than forty thousand gallons of "ardent spirits" were seized and destroyed, and there were more than seventeen thousand arrests over the course of Prohibition. Prominent bootleggers managed to escape notice of the agents more often than not, though their trunks riding low might have been a hint had anyone dared to arrest them. As Virginius Dabney wrote of the public's growing frustration with the law, "Bootleggers were riding around in Cadillacs while the public treasury suffered."[148]

RAIDS AND TRADE-OFFS

When Winston Churchill visited Richmond as the guest of Governor Harry F. Byrd during Prohibition, Admiral Cary T. Grayson warned the governor that his esteemed visitor would go through a quart of brandy a day. Byrd had nothing on hand but figured, quite rightly, that the publisher John Stewart Bryan would have a store, so he called him. The brandy appeared at the Executive Mansion. During the visit, Churchill was seen wandering around the mansion in his undershorts. Whether a quart was too much or too little, it's hard to say.[149]

Not everyone escaped the authorities. In 1930, police arrested two Jefferson Hotel employees, including the one with the keys to the storeroom, and charged them "with storing ardent spirits in violation of the State prohibition law. Both denied knowledge of the liquor and said that it belonged to guests. Police said they found three trunks containing two five-gallon kegs of whiskey, twenty six quarts and 41 pints of brands of liquor popular in pre-prohibition days."[150] Apparently, those brands were still popular.

In 1931, Chief Justice Charles Evans Hughes visited Richmond and wanted to stop by the grave site of the first chief justice, John Marshall, at Shockoe Hill Cemetery to place a wreath there. It was more than a little embarrassing when it became obvious that somebody was using the sarcophagus to store containers of bootleg whiskey.[151] Thankfully, Marshall always was fond of a drink.

Prohibition ended in Virginia in 1934, though the ban on liquor-by-the-drink stood in the commonwealth until 1968. The idea of what is a healthful drink is still open to debate, but Richmond has certainly come out of the desert of dryness and gotten all wet. With moonshine-infusing at Belle Isle

Moonshine; vodka at Cirrus; gin, rum, vodka and aquavit at James River Distilleries; bourbon, rye and wheat whiskey at Reservoir Distillery in Scott's Addition; mead at Black Heath Meadery; cider at Blue Bee and Buskey's; and more breweries than one can count sober, much less after visiting, it's just a tad ironic that the Temperance Fountain, a water fountain dedicated in Byrd Park in 1927 and intended to keep men from needing alcohol to wet their whistles, is dry.[152]

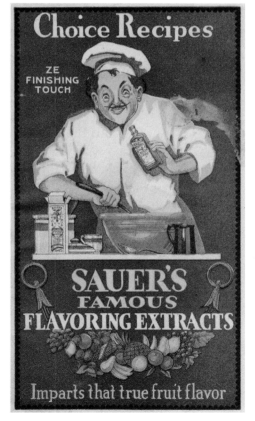

Above: The classic C.F. Sauer sign illuminated above the plant at 2000 West Broad Street. *Tommy McPhail, Big Spoon Agency.*

Left: The C.F. Sauer baker putting "ze finishing touch" on a 1915 recipe booklet. *Special Collections and Archives, VCU Libraries.*

The C.F. Sauer manufacturing plant, built in 1911. From a 1915 recipe booklet. *Special Collections and Archives, VCU Libraries.*

Quoit Club Punch. This one's waiting at the bar at The Roosevelt for you. *John Murden, The Roosevelt.*

Right: Vibrant catalogue covers from T.W. Wood & Sons inspired many a seed purchase. *Special Collections and Archives, VCU Libraries.*

Below: The Roosevelt on Church Hill at night. Bar manager Thomas Leggett put an updated version of Jasper Crouch's infamous punch on the menu (see chapter 24). *Justin Chesney, Fire, Flour & Fork.*

A beauty of an Atlantic sturgeon breaching on the James River during a Discover the James tour. *Don West.*

Matt Balazik (*left*), biologist at Virginia Commonwealth University's Rice Rivers Center, and assistant return a sturgeon to the James River after examining it. *Holly Smith.*

Drinks experts Robert Moss and Dave Wondrich expound on the wonders of punch in the John Marshall House basement during a special event. *Brandon Hambright, Fire, Flour & Fork.*

John Dabney descendant Jeremy Hardy at the first John Dabney Dinner held at Quirk Hotel during Fire, Flour & Fork. *Brandon Hambright, FFF.*

Richmond sculptor Edward Valentine's Carrara marble statue of Thomas Jefferson in the Palm Court of the Jefferson Hotel. *Sarah Hauser, Virginia Tourism Corporation (Virginia.org).*

A view of Richmond across the James River from Manchester. *Special Collections and Archives, VCU Libraries.*

The Jefferson reopened in 1907 after extensive renovations and was able to host the Virginia Hotel Association convention soon after. *Buttolph Collection, New York Public Library.*

Left: Some of Richmond's finest chefs put these squash blossom stunners from Manakintowne on their menus in the summer. *Manakintowne Specialty Growers.*

Below: An eye-popping display of tomato varieties available from Manakintowne, a pioneer of locally grown produce with the emphasis on flavor. *Jo Pendergraph, Manakintowne Specialty Growers.*

A circa 1932 Eskimo Pie ad in a Reynolds Metals company report. Wrapping the treats in foil was an early innovation. *Eskimo Pie Corp.*

Vendors show off their wares at Sixth Street Market in the early 1900s. *Special Collections and Archives, VCU Libraries.*

Above: Manakintowne's Tonic No. 1 is packed with homegrown Espelette peppers, cider vinegar and sea salt. *Fire, Flour & Fork*.

Left: The Famous Foods of Virginia sign and water tower still stand at the Cookie Lofts. *Susan Winiecki*.

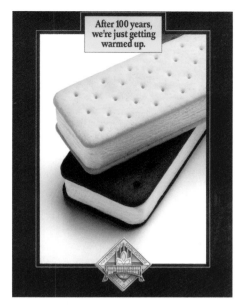

After 100 years, we're just getting warmed up.

Left: The cookie base for ice cream sandwiches is an Interbake standard. *Interbake Foods.*

Below: La Milpa's Day of the Dead celebration is colorful, to say the least. *David James, La Milpa.*

Richmond artist Ed Trask's mural brightens the streetscape outside Ellwood Thompson's in Carytown. *Ellwood Thompson's.*

A very green selection of Amy's Organic fall produce for sale at a market. *Brandon Hambright, Fire, Flour & Fork.*

Reservoir Distillery in Scott's Addition is just one of many craft spirit makers in Richmond after that dry spell known as Prohibition. *Nicole Martorana, Fire, Flour & Fork.*

Climax and Truade ads in the 1950s—the former carbonated and homegrown, the other non-carbonated and just bottled here. *Edith Shelton, Edith K. Shelton Photograph Collection, The Valentine.*

FFV Lemon Wafers tin. Note Southern Biscuit Company at bottom. *Justin Vaughan, Collection of Kathy Emerson.*

Pat and Betty, aka Pat Schweitzer and Betty Morton of Reynolds Test Kitchen fame, in their trademark white coats. *Collection of Pat Schweitzer.*

The Sally Bell's Kitchen sign hangs over SBK's new location on West Broad Street. Note the James Beard Foundation logo. *Maureen Egan.*

This Uneeda Biscuit advertisement from the National Biscuit Company gives the wall across Twenty-Fifth Street from St. John's Church a little flavor. *Maureen Egan.*

Clearly a post-Prohibition venture, on Jefferson Street across from Comfort, which happens to have an excellent whiskey assortment. *Maureen Egan.*

CHAPTER 16

SALLY BELL'S BEGINNINGS

The Woman's Exchange

The twenty-one concerned and community-minded women from several Presbyterian churches who founded the Richmond Exchange for Woman's Work in March 1883 to "aid ladies whose pecuniary circumstances require them to make their own handiwork a means of support" could not have imagined the good works, better food and great deal of money that the Exchange would contribute to the community in its seventy-two-year history. It even served as midwife to the birth of a Richmond institution, Sally Bell's Kitchen, that went on to receive a James Beard America's Classic Award in 2015. More on that later.

WOMEN AT WORK

Headquartered at the corner of Third and East Franklin Streets, the Exchange (later renamed the Woman's Exchange) was modeled after organizations in Brooklyn, New York City and New Orleans "to assist needy gentlewomen" who sought income and had a talent for food preparation, knitting, sewing or other handiwork. At the time, such gentlewomen had few respectable options for supporting themselves or their families. In the early days of the enterprise, women reportedly delivered their goods to the Exchange at night or under veils so they wouldn't be recognized. What began with a sense of shame became a source of pride and an engine of home economics at its most basic form as buyers flocked to the Exchange

Women in the Exchange Salesroom at 300 East Franklin Street. *The Valentine.*

to purchase sought-after delicacies such as terrapin stew, beaten biscuits, brandied peaches and iced Lady Baltimore cake.[153]

The Exchange was an administrative marvel, with Mrs. S.H. Hawes serving as president for umpteen years. Three vice presidents, two secretaries, a treasurer and more than thirty prominent Richmond women on the board of managers, not to mention an advisory board of a few husbands—all in volunteer capacity—assisted. A paid superintendent, for its first twenty years Miss Frances E. Munford, vetted the potential consignors in conjunction with the appropriate committees. Handiwork such as lace, linen, children's clothing and all manner of pickles, rolls, jams, pies and cakes were sold at the Salesroom at 300 East Franklin Street. Many items, including lobster a la Newburg, chicken croquettes and dozens of other dishes, could be special ordered for teas and luncheons.[154]

QUALITY CONTROL

The organization's handbook had many rules to live by, including "no limitations or restrictions which would, in effect, exclude any class of needy females. It enjoins no conditions except requiring a standard of excellence in all articles placed on sale." Regrettably, it is likely that women of color were excluded, given the stubborn segregation of the time and that Virginia Randolph felt the need to start her own exchange for black women. (See chapter 17.)

The ladies were strict about the quality of goods accepted, and the handbook intoned that the Salesroom Committee "will confer with Superintendent in regard to doubtful consignors, and decide as to their worthiness." Furthermore, "Committees are instructed to accept or refuse work upon its own merits, not allowing critical judgment to be influenced by sympathy. Especially is this true in the Domestic Department, where every variety of cake, preserved fruits, pickles, etc. are kept constantly on hand."[155]

Munford must have had a keen eye and reliable taste buds because the Exchange had a reputation for high quality. In one early year, 455 out of 555 domestic jars brought to the Salesroom sold.

To ensure freshness, there was Rule 14: "Pickles, preserves and jellies are sampled every year, and cannot be received before Oct. 1st and after April 1st." And as the women on the sales floor were not the makers of the food for sale, a modification of the rules was in order: "In order to make intelligent sales, it will be necessary that there be an understanding between the Superintendent and the consignor of mixed pickles or other articles compounded of different things, as to ingredients."[156]

To fund the operation, initially 10 percent of the sales price went to the Exchange, and the board members paid dues and fees if they couldn't do their assigned shifts managing the organization. They occasionally held cooking demonstrations and offered luncheons as fundraisers for the paying public to draw them to the Salesroom.

At its peak, the Exchange had six hundred consignors, and in its first thirty-four years, it paid $334,000 to hundreds of women, helping them pay for school for their children or provide care for an invalid mother. One consignor wrote she "could not hold her home together without the Exchange."[157]

With women more easily incorporated in the workforce and health department regulations for food preparation becoming onerous, the Exchange closed for good in June 1955. For seventy-two years, its members had provided top-quality goods and provided many women the means to help themselves and their families. Several businesses trace their roots to the Exchange, including Mrs. Fearnow's Brunswick Stew, the Mixing Bowl and the aforementioned Sally Bell's Kitchen, a James Beard America's Classic Award winner.

WHEN ELIZABETH MET SALLIE

In 1924, Sarah "Sallie" Cabell Jones, bookkeeper for the Exchange, and Elizabeth Lee Milton, who made a mean devil's food cake that she sold there, decided they could make a go of it on their own. They outfitted a spot at Grace and Pine Streets and focused on a wholesale business, calling it Sarah Lee Kitchen, combining parts of their names. Their recipes (in a little red notebook), most often purchased at bakeries and markets around the city, contributed to many a picnic, luncheon, dinner party and holiday gathering.[158]

When Milton moved to New York in 1929, Jones bought her out and decided it was time to concentrate on the retail side of the business. The cooks and bakers in the back continued to make everything, including the mayonnaise, every day. One busy day, the pace was slowed by the absence of a regular girl. Jones sent her deliveryman to the girl's apartment, but she wasn't there. Estelle Curtis was. She was all of sixteen years old. She said she'd be willing to help that day, and she became the longest-serving employee of the kitchen, learning to bake everything and make all the salads

Sarah Lee Kitchen

701 W. Grace Street
Madison 6281
Richmond, Va.

Fruit Cakes, Plum Pudd-
ing made from famous
family recipes

Cakes for the home, par-
ties and holiday
occasions

Pastries

Breads—Salt-risen, Whole Wheat,
Sally Lunn and Bran Muffins
Cheese Straws

Above: Sarah Lee Kitchen advertisement from *Virginia Cookery*, Virginia League of Women Voters cookbook long before Sara Lee bought the rights to the name. *Special Collections and Archives, VCU.*

Right: The founder of the feast, Sarah Cabell Jones. *Sally Bell's Kitchen.*

in her sixty years of devoted work. Eventually, her daughter came to work, as did her grandson Billy Thompson after Curtis retired.[159] Thompson is a special case, one of the few males to work in the kitchen over the years, a jack-of-all-trades. Over the decades, women, both black and white, have worked together even while the city around them was segregated, in the kitchen improving recipes and singing during the long prep hours and at the counter, boxing up orders for regular customers.

By 1951, Jones had moved the kitchen to 708 West Grace Street and had apartments made upstairs for herself and her brother's family. In the same decade, they had a protracted back-and-forth with attorneys for Sara Lee's of Chicago demanding that the Richmond business stop using the name Sarah Lee Kitchen. Jones was not one to wilt under pressure. She argued that Sarah Lee had been around since 1924, in Virginia and out-of-state with mail orders, trademarked and all. The companies eventually agreed that Sarah Lee Kitchen would sell in Virginia and Sara Lee's would not. Soon enough though, Sara Lee products were in a nearby Safeway, and once again Jones came up against a powerful force. Sara Lee wanted to be a national player and demanded the name free and clear. In 1959, on the advice of her nephew, Jones finally accepted a settlement from Sara Lee in exchange for letting go of the name Sarah Lee Kitchen.[160]

A New Look

The classic Sally Bell's sign that hung above the 708 West Grace Street location for decades. *Nicole Martorana, Fire, Flour & Fork.*

She christened the new business Sally Bell's Kitchen, using a version of her nickname and the "bell" from her middle name Cabell. An updated logo so familiar now on the white pasteboard lunchboxes sealed the deal. That ordeal over, Jones started to think about the next phase of the business.

She hoped to convince her nephews and nieces to buy it from her, but no one bit. Jones had a deal with a young couple in the late '60s, but after one day at the helm, they turned in the keys to her and said running the business wasn't for them after all. Soon after, she was able to convince her nephew Hunter and his wife, Marcyne Jones, to take over, and Sally Bell's made the transition to

Jay Turner of Sally Bell's shows off a tray of the famous cupcakes that are iced upside down. *Susan Winiecki.*

the second generation. Marcyne's daughter Sarah and her son Scott and his wife, Martha Jones, became more involved in the 1980s. Now Martha Jones is the Jones woman you'll see working at Sally Bell's along with so many familiar faces at the counter and in the back.[161]

It's not as if nothing changed over the decades. Sally Bell's used to get whole coconuts from a nearby supplier that had its own grater, which worked well for the coconut cakes, a holiday favorite. When that was no longer available, they smashed coconuts outside on the sidewalk and inside with hammers. Great-nieces and nephews of the founder continued to pay their dues working at the shop, so the fourth generation has played its part.[162]

INDUSTRIOUS WOMEN

The Southern Foodways Alliance, which studies and celebrates southern food and culture, became so smitten with Sally Bell's that it commissioned a film, *Boxed Lunch*, by Richmonders Nicole Lang and Christophile Konstas, for its 2013 Field Trip to Richmond. It's a sweet film, well worth a watch online to see the obscure Richmond tradition of people lining up at 6:00

A roll of Sally Bell's box-tying ribbon from an earlier era. *Susan Winiecki.*

a.m. in front of Sally Bell's on Christmas Eve for potato salad. And to hear Marcyne Jones chuckle, "I've had people cry because they couldn't get a deviled egg."[163]

As fast food has changed American diets and habits, and every road leads to the same ole, same ole, Sally Bell's has become a darling of the food press and anyone who appreciates a fresh sandwich and a cupcake iced upside down so the frosting wraps around it. (Get the mocha chocolate!) Everything old is new again after more than ninety years. And admired. In 2015, Sally Bell's Kitchen received a James Beard America's Classic Award, "given to regional establishments, often family-owned, that are treasured for their quality food, local character, and lasting appeal." Scott and Martha Jones picked it up in Chicago that May.

The award citation read:

> *Sally Bell's is a take-away operation. Step to the counter and order a chicken salad or egg salad sandwich, among a number of other options. The counterwoman will hand over your prize in a white pasteboard box, tied with twine. Inside will be a paper cup of potato salad or macaroni salad, a deviled egg half wrapped in tissue, a cheese wafer crowned with a pecan, and a cupcake enrobed in glaze. All will taste like someone's grandmother made them. Nine decades after it first opened, Sally Bell's still excels at handmade goods prepared by industrious women.*[164]

Miss Sarah Cabell Jones would have been proud. And the Woman's Exchange should take a bow.

In late 2016, Sally Bell's moved off Grace Street to new digs at 2337 West Broad Street that somehow re-create the feel of 708 West Grace. There's more room for customers to line up at the counter with all the familiar faces behind it. There's even seating for thirty-six to sit and enjoy lunch (or a cupcake). That the space still feels like you're stepping into a place your grandmother or great-grandmother would feel at home in is a testament to Scott Jones's work painting the familiar colonial blue and installing the black-and-white floor that echoes the similarly hued checked paper that lines every cardboard box. The founders' recipes are still in use. The red notebook still holds the secrets. The mayonnaise still gets made every morning.

The quintessential Richmond article is a Sally Bell's boxed lunch. It's what should be in a Richmond time capsule, but why waste the tastes? Bite into Richmond history instead.

CHAPTER 17

THE HENRICO PLAN

Virginia Randolph

A child must learn how to use his hands.
There is no use for a mind if you can't use your hands.[165]

The destiny of our race depends, largely, upon the training children receive
in the classroom, and how careful we should be.[166]

Rising at 4:30 a.m. on Sundays, Virginia Estelle Randolph, a teacher and mother, would bake bread before heading to church at Moore Street Baptist. She also would bake every day during the school week.

Actually, Randolph made bread seven days a week, putting a small "for sale" sign on her door at 817 West Marshall Street. That pin money went to support the fourteen "adopted" children who lived with her and toward the school named after her on Mountain Road in Henrico County.[167]

"Of course, I was always in debt. I never had any money," she told the *Richmond Times-Dispatch* in a June 8, 1947 story.[168]

At times, she even disassembled her neighbor's still-warm stove and brought it to class so she could teach cooking lessons to her "scholars" during the day and home economics courses to their mothers at night.[169]

A teacher since the age of sixteen, Randolph created the Henrico Plan, a program for African American students in rural areas that combined academic subjects with vocational ones—cooking, gardening, masonry, woodworking and sewing; a program that was replicated as far away as Africa; a program that initially received criticism from parents who threatened her job.[170]

Virginia Randolph on the steps of the old Mountain Road School. *The Jackson Davis Collection of African American Photographs, Albert and Shirley Small Collections Library, University of Virginia.*

After the Civil War, separate public schools for African Americans were usually overcrowded and in abysmal condition. Young African American women who were poor but talented had limited options, other than teaching, to improve themselves and their communities. These teachers included Chesterfield's Ora Brown Stokes, Richmond's Maggie Lena Walker and, of course, Randolph and her sister, Emma Randolph Washington.[171]

WORKING THE SYSTEM

Her industrial teaching approach followed that of Hampton Institute graduate Booker T. Washington. He was at odds with W.E.B. Du Bois, who declared industrial education as "fundamentally false" and wanted to provide African Americans with a classical education that would prepare students for higher education and professions.[172]

"Booker T. Washington and Virginia Randolph knew how to work the system," said historian Dr. Lauranett Lee. "They understood where they could get support and do what they could to get that support."[173]

Born the second daughter of four to former slaves Sarah Carter and Nelson Randolph, Randolph lost her father, a bricklayer, when she was a

Niece Aretha Randolph's donation to the school stitched into a circa 1900 log cabin–style quilt at the Virginia Randolph Museum. *Susan Winiecki.*

toddler.[174] Her mother, who kept house for a university professor, taught her to cook, sew and knit in their one-room house on Henry Street. Randolph graduated from the Richmond Normal and High School and passed the Henrico County teachers' examination at sixteen. She initially took a job teaching in Goochland County, but in 1894, she was appointed a teacher of a one-room school with fourteen enrolled students on Mountain Road. By the end of the school year, the enrollment had increased to eighty.[175]

She described her school as "bare within, bare without,"[176] so she formed a "Willing Workers Club," an early PTA, to help her raise funds to cover such things as gravel for a walkway leading to the school. A quilt with the who's who of Richmond and their embroidered names and gravel donation amounts equaling $110 was one of their projects. The city's future newspaper publisher John S. Bryan donated $5, and Randolph's own niece Aretha gave $1.[177]

While organized rural, vocational education didn't come to white students until the passage of the Smith-Lever Act in 1914, Randolph saw its combination with academics as crucial for her students twenty years earlier.[178]

DOUBLE DUTY

Randolph was living amid dynamic minds—scholars at the nearby Hartshorn Memorial College for African American women (the first black women's college to confer bachelor's degrees), professors at Virginia Union University and the pastor of her own church, Gordon B. Hancock, who also taught at VUU and preached the power of "Double-Duty Dollar." Hancock meant that dollars spent with African American businesses that hired African American employees advanced the community overall. Those influences underpinned Randolph's belief that she had to feed her students' minds and fill their hands with skills.[179]

So impressed with what Randolph had been doing on Mountain Road for nearly fifteen years, Henrico School superintendent Jackson T. Davis applied for her to become one of the Jeanes Foundation–supported Industrial School Supervisors at forty dollars per month in 1908. For nine months, she traveled and visited twenty-two other African American schools throughout the state and provided teacher training. She visited schools in North Carolina and Georgia, too.[180]

In 1915, a four-room frame school was built, and it opened as the Virginia E. Randolph Training School. While Randolph took many students into her home, a dormitory for students and teachers was needed. Randolph and other teachers pooled their money and purchased a piece of property for $1,000. The dormitory opened in 1924.[181]

Henrico, by 1916, had eighteen industrial colored schools, catering to students and adults, along with fifty gardens and 125 students in poultry and canning clubs. To support these efforts, in the *Times-Dispatch* Sunday Feature section on July 16, Superintendent J.D. Harris announced Randolph's creation of a Colored Industrial Exchange on West Broad Street where products would be sold:

I want also to speak of the colored work in the county. Henrico has one of the ablest colored supervisors in the person of Virginia Randolph. There are about 50 members of the canning club and 75 in the poultry club. These negro boys and girls are raising pure-bred Plymouth Rocks only. Reports coming into this office show that they have over 700 chickens, and I am sure they will make a creditable exhibit at the State Fair. Virginia Randolph has established what is known as a Colored Industrial Exchange on Broad Street, where, the products of the canning club and the poultry club will be marketed. This Colored Industrial Exchange is meeting a long-felt want in the life of the colored people of Henrico, and it is the intention of Virginia Randolph to so develop this marketing feature that instead of 50 gardens, here will be 5,000 among the old and the young whose products will go through this exchange. The progress of this work in Henrico is only measured by the amount of money available to take care of it. We hope by another year to be in a position to extend the work along other lines.[182]

Tragedy struck in 1929. The 1915 school building and the original one-room schoolhouse were destroyed by fire. But a brick building of eight

Cooking students at the Mountain Road School. *The Jackson Davis Collection of African American Photographs, Albert and Shirley Small Collections Library, University of Virginia.*

Cakes and canned goods made by students were sold at the Industrial Exchange on Broad Street. *The Jackson Davis Collection of African American Photographs, Albert and Shirley Small Collections Library, University of Virginia.*

rooms, a small library and auditorium was built a year later with assistance from Julius Rosenwald, president of Sears Roebuck Company.[183]

The school grew again in 1937 when a separate home economics cottage was built. This brick Cape Cod–style house later became Randolph's office. Randolph retired in 1949 after fifty-seven years of service and passed away in 1958.[184]

Today, the brick home economics cottage houses the compact but powerful Virginia Randolph Museum. Don't miss the glass-ensconced congratulatory cake sent to Randolph in 1927. The cake looks like an oversize Western Union telegram. It's priceless, as is the Virginia Randolph Foundation, which began awarding scholarships annually in 1956. The first recipient, Elwood Johnson Thornton III, received his award from Randolph herself.[185]

As the industrial schools supervisor, Randolph was what we call today an education specialist, according to former school superintendent Dr. William C. Bosher Jr. "A specialist who could help plant these seeds of curriculum.… She was an evangelist for technical education."[186]

CHAPTER 18

"GROWING GIRLS"

Ella Agnew and Tomato Clubs

I, Susan Winiecki, have Ella Graham Agnew to thank for my middle school 4-H memories—making a zippered sleeveless shift that I had to model in the Erie County Fair fashion show in Western New York. While I may have dreaded it at the time, learning to sew and then showing off my product instilled confidence.

Agnew, at age thirty-nine—after running a girls' school in South Africa and working for the YWCA in Ohio—returned to Richmond and took a job establishing Girls Tomato Clubs across the state in 1910. These canning clubs were the Progressive movement's attempt to modernize rural life and the beginnings of 4-H and home economics classes throughout the country. For Agnew, this was her way of paving more educational avenues for women.[187]

IMPROVING EDUCATION

At the YWCA in Toledo, a young girl had come into Agnew's office complaining about how poor her high school education was. She had been encouraged to stay in school so that she would be better able to find a job. However, when she applied for positions after graduation, she was told that she was not equipped for work.[188]

What Agnew wanted was an opportunity to improve education and expand options for girls in the United States. In South Africa where she had taught, girls also were expected to take some sort of sewing or handiwork class in addition to their studies.

Virginia was the first state to introduce cooperative extension work for women through its state board of education. That program became part of a larger federal initiative in 1915 that set up agricultural instruction for men, home demonstration (economics) education for women and 4-H Clubs for children—Head. Heart. Hand. Health. Land-grant university Virginia Tech eventually took over the program in 1920, and Hampton Institute ran the program for African Americans.[189]

"While doing the work, I felt that I was not only growing tomatoes and vegetables, but also growing girls," Agnew told the *Richmond News Leader* in 1953.[190]

GROWING PAINS

Upon becoming the country's first female home demonstration agent, Agnew, who grew up in rural Nottoway County, had never planted or canned, and she told her boss that. "If you're looking for a person totally ignorant of the work, I'm the person." He replied, "But you know girls, Miss Agnew, and they are much harder to learn than tomatoes."[191]

And that sent her in search of agricultural coaching, which she eventually found at the African American Hampton Institute, since no other school would enroll women at the time.[192] And she used her family's farm in Nottoway as a "laboratory," figuring out how to raise and can tomatoes.[193]

When she began traversing the state in July 1910, there were a handful of good roads, no automobiles and few rural telephones. She would go by horse and buggy or by farm wagon. Or she just walked to schools and homes in Halifax and Nottoway Counties, where the first two clubs were established. At the time, the notion of educational clubs for white female students organized and run by women was a bit scandalous, so Agnew often heard untoward comments. And for the first four years, Agnew also had to find ways to match half the funds given to her by the state to run each program.[194]

At a Fourth of July picnic in 1910 in Halifax, Agnew did not have a receptive crowd: "Here I stood in an empty wagon body and spoke to a mixed group of about 600 men and women to the horror of many of the people present. I may add, to my own horror, for my knees were shaking and to this day I remember not one word I said—but I did hear an outraged woman say, 'no self-respecting would'—I moved away."[195]

Ella Agnew took her Tomato Club girls to a conference in South Carolina in 1913. *Ella Graham Agnew Papers, circa 1846–1992. Accession 42285. Girls Canning Club photograph, folder Box 2, folder 19, personal papers collection, the Library of Virginia.*

During another round of travel, she faced discrimination when trying to check her baggage at a train station. She had two bags filled with cans for her projects that a train station employee refused to accept. Then, a carpenter came by and checked a large box. She asked why he couldn't check hers. They are tools of his trade, the checker told her. She placed the two bags of cans on the rack and told him, "These are the tools of my trade and walked off."[196]

Despite the initial chilly receptions, clubs were established and thrived. At the 1913 state fair with her charges, Agnew recalled huge tomato stands that held displays of canned tomatoes and catsup made by the canning groups. "The day after the fair, a funeral was held to bury the cans that had spoiled or blown up during the occasion. Bounding in buggies on the way to the fair and then sitting in the heat was too much for the rural tomatoes. They blew up." And to "the tomato cemetery" they went, according to her memoirs.[197]

Growing in popularity, the home demonstration work was eventually separated into two groups: 4-H Clubs for girls and home demonstration clubs for women. (Thirty years later, in 1946, the 4-H Clubs had eighteen thousand student members and the home demonstration clubs had thirty-one thousand women across Virginia.)[198]

In between her home demonstration work throughout the state, Agnew also was involved in the creation of the Virginia Federation of Business and Professional Women's Clubs and became its first president in 1919. Members included Pin Money Pickles' founder Ellen Kidd and the Rosegill Tea Room's owner, Mrs. Horace Welford Jones.[199]

Agnew resigned from her state position as "assistant director of extension in charge of women's work" in 1921 and took a job with the national YWCA board in New York, traveling the country and studying ways for rural communities to raise money to establish chapters. "No person is large enough to have a program built around her personality—that work must go on without her," Agnew said.[200]

New Rows to Hoe

Agnew returned to Richmond and became an editor at *Southern Planter* magazine, founded in 1841. She changed the name of her section from the women's department to the home department because she believed that the home belongs to the man as well as the woman. While at *Southern Planter*, she passed tests that enabled her to become a member of both the Newspaper Institute of America and the American Landscape Association.

She stayed in that editorial position for five years before being named a director with the Federal Emergency Relief Organization, overseeing women's relief, in 1933. This agency eventually became the Works Progress Administration. One of her efforts included the revival of the flax industry in the Eastern Shore by a group of women.[201]

This was the most challenging work I had ever undertaken. Our greatest job was to help people appreciate and recognize the fact that they were out of a job through no fault of their own....I spent millions of dollars per month right here in Richmond. It was the taxpayer's money, and Richmond people never asked me how I spent it, but they never hesitated to criticize the work I was doing. As long as people don't criticize you, you are not accomplishing anything.[202]

Ella Agnew was the first female editor at the *Southern Planter*. *Ella Graham Agnew Papers, circa 1846–1992. Accession 42285, folder Box 2, folder 17, personal papers collection, Library of Virginia.*

Upon her retirement, a Washington official quoted in the *Virginia Home Economics Association's News Letter* succinctly summed up Agnew's career: "The outstanding characteristic that comes to mind when considering Miss Agnew's public service career is the courage with which she tackled new ideas and new programs, her indifference to the fact it has never been done before."[203]

CHAPTER 19

THE LAST WORD IN VIRGINIA DAINTIES

The Tearoom of Fannie Jones

The concept of a southern tearoom was entirely foreign to me—a Polish-American kid from Western New York—until I took a job with Richmond Newspapers Inc. in downtown Richmond in the late 1980s. Literally within four blocks of the newspaper building, in either direction, was a tearoom: homey Mrs. Morton's to the west, where you filled out your own order ticket, and fashionable Miller & Rhoads to the east, with its runway shows, women in Sara Sue hats and Eddie Weaver at the organ. A little farther west, at 900 West Franklin, was the Chesterfield Tea Room, which opened in 1903 but catered primarily to men and women living in the Chesterfield Apartments. At the time, it was considered the longest continuously serving establishment in the city.[204]

Between the yeast rolls at Mrs. Morton's and the Missouri Club and chocolate silk pie at Miller & Rhoads, I needed my downtown YMCA membership more than ever. But by 1991, all three tearooms were closed, leaving us with memories and, luckily, a few recipes.

A ROOM OF THEIR OWN

Jan Whitaker, author of *Tea at the Blue Lantern Inn: A Social History of the Tea Craze in America*, shared that most tearooms were owned or managed by women. "Almost everyone from schoolteachers to recent college graduates to homemakers wanted to run one. In the 1920s especially, tea rooms became the fashionable places for women to meet friends in small towns, big cities and suburbs alike."[205]

This entrepreneurial spirit was linked to the women's suffrage movement in the 1910s as well as to the expansion of educational and work opportunities for women. Add in the advent of the automobile, and women needed places to meet.

By 1916 in Richmond, the Rosegill Tea Room was that place, located at 20 West Franklin and run by Fannie Jones. She and her husband, a druggist, lived in Newport News at the turn of the century but had moved to Richmond by 1910. Fannie, who was then forty-eight, was operating a boardinghouse at 200 East Franklin Street filled with twenty-four guests, including men, women and children.[206]

Her advertising in 1911 read, "First-class accommodations for permanent, transient and table boarders can be secured with Mrs. Horace Welford Jones at 200 E. Franklin. Gentlemen a specialty."[207]

Soon after, Jones was widowed and moved to 20 West Franklin. Although she had fewer boarders living with her there, she opened a tearoom that was open to the public. Jones touted afternoon tea with waffles and muffins

A postcard image of Fannie Jones's boardinghouse at 200 East Franklin Street. *The* Shockoe Examiner *and Ray Bonis.*

Rosegill Tea Room
(Mrs. Horace Welford Jones)

20 West Franklin Street
Richmond, Va.

A 1921 ad for the Rosegill Tea Room, owned by Fannie Jones, in the *Virginia Cookery* cookbook, which she chaired for the new Virginia League of Women Voters. *Susan Winiecki.*

and began marketing the Rosegill as "The Last Word in Virginia Dainties" with tempting luncheons, dinners and small tables.[208]

Jones also was one of the hostesses of a June 1919 Jefferson Hotel luncheon, during which the first statewide group for women in business—Virginia Federation of Business and Professional Women's Club—was formed and appointed Ella Agnew its first president.[209]

By 1921, Jones also was involved with the newly formed Virginia League of Women Voters. After the Nineteenth Amendment became law in 1920 and the Equal Suffrage League of Virginia morphed into the nonpartisan voters' league, an ad for the Rosegill appeared in that organization's 1921 *Virginia Cookery Book*, with Jones serving as the project's "general chairman."

To demonstrate its interest in the question of Food Supply and Demand:
To demonstrate further that the woman voter is none the less the efficient housewife:
The Virginia League of Women Voters offers this book of Virginia Cookery in the hope that those who use it will find it helpful and will have the added satisfaction of knowing that by purchasing a copy they will have contributed to the fund of the League for education in good citizenship....Each recipe is tested. Many have been in families for several generations. All are good.[210]

The book also included a poignant dedication to one of the founders of the state suffrage league, Lila Meade Valentine, who died in 1921: "our valiant pioneer for the enfranchisement of Virginia women, who saw the potentiality of unshackled womanhood."

MIXING IT UP

Helping run the Rosegill Tea Room kitchen for Jones was an African American cook, Nannie Robinson, who had been working at the restaurant for decades when the tearoom went up for sale in 1948.

That's the year Samuel E. and Julia Bell Morton arrived in town, looking for their own Richmond restaurant, building upon Sam's experience managing a cafeteria in Charlottesville. They saw an ad in the paper that said, "For Rent—Tea Room on Franklin St." They purchased the Rosegill and ran it for four years, with Sam learning how to the make the famous yeast rolls from Robinson.

The Mortons then moved down the street, buying the 1886 Bosher house at 2 East Franklin Street at the corner of Foushee Street in 1952. They opened Mrs. Morton's Tea Room there.[211]

For nearly thirty years, Julia Morton worked downtown, serving as hostess of the restaurant that bore her name, but lived in Ashland. After her husband passed away in the fall of 1980, she and her daughter moved into the upstairs quarters on Franklin, and Morton finally learned to make the famous rolls. By November 1981, after about twenty-five Franklin Street zoning battles with the city, she decided to temporarily close Mrs. Morton's and challenge Henry W. "Chuck" Richardson for his city council seat, but was defeated. "It's been a lot of fun. It's tiring, but not as tiring as working in the tearoom for 16 hours," she told Steve Clark of the *Richmond News Leader* about her council race.[212]

Mrs. Morton's Tea Room reopened in 1983 and continued feeding fans of its chicken and, of course, Nannie Robinson's rolls until the restaurant closed on July 16, 1991. It served 375 rolls that day, made by Marsha Cox, the wife of Mrs. Morton's nephew Leo Morton Cox.[213]

The following month, the *Richmond Times-Dispatch* held a contest, seeking recipes for rolls that were closest to those originally made by Nannie Robinson. More than 110 entries were received, and 5 were chosen finalists and printed in the paper.[214]

Julia Morton passed away in December 1991. A roll recipe used by Fannie Jones is printed in the last chapter of this book.

CHAPTER 20

CONVEYING SUCCESS

FFV and the Girl Scouts

I n September 2016, the eighteen-foot water tower atop the former Famous Foods of Virginia (FFV) cookie factory got a contemporary makeover by muralist Mickael Broth.[215] It was, in a way, the cherry on top of this $24 million adaptive reuse of a 185,000-square-foot landmark manufacturing site along Broad Street, just blocks from the former 1916 Putney Shoe factory, the former J.H. Jenkins Publishing House and the still very much alive and well C.F. Sauer spice and extract plant, which opened in 1911.[216]

The FFV factory, which opened in 1927 and closed in 2006, had five ovens—they could produce up to 640,000 cookies in an hour—and it was the first cookie company to use aluminum foil in its packaging. By 2014, the historic landmark had been converted into 178 apartments. These Cookie Loft Apartments now serve as an anchor to the burgeoning Scott's Addition retail and dining district across the street.[217]

MADE-IN-RICHMOND BISCUITS

The factory's story begins in 1899, when the Southern Biscuit Works was created and backed by some of the biggest names in Richmond business: J.S. Brockenbrough, T.C. Williams Jr., R.S. Bosher and J.J. Montague. Production began on March 6, 1900, with seventy-five employees, on Byrd Street between Fifth and Sixth Streets in what was the former Alleghany Box factory.[218] The *Richmond Times* reported, "Crackers by the Car Load," but the company soon faced a setback when a fire ripped through the factory on May 23. The building, which was fully insured, had to be rebuilt.[219]

The company's popularity really took off with its Sailor Boy Pilot Bread, an unleavened cracker with no salt on top akin to hardtack, which it began producing in 1919. That product is still sold today, though 98 percent of what's produced is sold in Alaska.[220]

A 1921 ad for the Old Dutch Market at Seventh and Franklin Streets touts a Saturday demonstration with products from Southern Biscuit and the ability to buy a pound of seven different varieties for twenty-five cents: "Buy made-in-Richmond biscuits and be assured of their freshness."

MONUMENT TO MAKERS

When the Southern Biscuit Works moved to its new six-story factory, described by executives as a "monument to the industry of the company," it also changed its name to the Southern Biscuit Co. and began putting out products under the FFV label, becoming a national brand. At that time, the company was producing more than one hundred varieties of crackers and cakes.[221]

Southern Biscuit Works' factory. *Interbake Foods.*

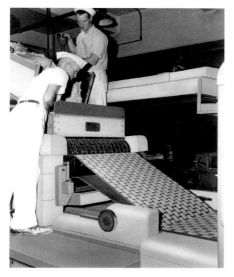

Left: Cracker production in 1940. *Interbake Foods.*

Right: The Southern Biscuit Company became an official baker of Girl Scout cookies in 1937. It also began marketing products under the FFV label. *Interbake Foods.*

Southern Biscuit really hit its stride through baking for other entities. One such marriage began in 1937 with the Girl Scouts. The company became a licensed Girl Scout cookie baker and continues to this day under ABC Bakers of Interbake Foods, LLC, which is today's iteration of Southern Biscuit and is still headquartered in Richmond.[222] The company never tried to be flashy or be on the cutting edge of the next new thing (remember the soft cookie rage, anyone?). It stuck to its FFV classics, to niche cookie and cracker production and to chocolate "dairy product wafer" production for ice cream sandwich makers.[223]

What customers all over the country remember now about FFV are such favorites as lemon thins, orange thins, shortbread, coconut macaroon snow creams, colonial girl sandwich and chocolate pecans. By the 1950s, these cookies stayed "nine times fresher," according to ads, because of the aluminum foil packaging. The thins had a cult-like following, but the company eventually stopped producing them because too many broke before coming out of the box.[224]

"With our product line, we want to be where the big guys aren't," Raymond A. Baxter, Interbake's president and chief executive officer, told the *Richmond News Leader* in 1989. He had come to Interbake after working for Frito-Lay.[225]

Interbake ovens in Richmond could produce up to 640,000 cookies in an hour. *Interbake Foods.*

"We've survived for 90 years because we make a good quality cookie, and we never compromised on that....We all know each other here, and it is a fun business. After all, we sell cookies. We can't take ourselves too seriously."[226]

If you are lucky, you can come across an old FFV Lemon Thin tin in Richmond antique malls, complete with a drawing of that six-story cookie factory. It was a perfect gift for a friend who moved into an apartment there last year. Now she has to find a recipe for lemon thins to put inside.

CHAPTER 21

HULL STREET OPPORTUNITIES

From Ukrop's to La Milpa

We strive to lead by example and with a single mission:
To treat others the way you want to be treated.
—*Bobby Ukrop*

Richmond's pre–Civil War population was far more than descendants of the first English families of Virginia and enslaved African Americans, which is mind-bending to some who have only envisioned the antebellum South depicted in movies.

At First African Baptist Church, free blacks attended with those who were enslaved. German and Irish immigrants were a large part of our merchant class and workforce, looking for economic opportunities that weren't available for them in their countries. An 1856 city map shows a German Catholic church, two synagogues and two African Baptist churches—along with two public markets, slave jails and four railroad depots.[227] One young Irish American living in Richmond lifted his glass at a Fourth of July celebration in 1852 and used the toast: "The land we live in; not forgetting the land we left."[228]

FROM HUNGARY TO HERE

Another wave of immigrants arrived at the turn of the century. Once again, they came to better their circumstances; they came for jobs; they came for land. In 1910, a group of Slovak families moved to Henrico County from Pennsylvania. By 1913, they had established the First Slovak Baptist Church in eastern Henrico County in the area of Glendale. Stefan Ukrop was part of a group that donated three acres of land on which to build the church, dedicated in 1914.[229] Stefan, born in 1876 in Dobrá Niva, Hungary, arrived in the United States in 1901 and initially settled near Pittsburgh.

In Henrico, Stefan and his wife, Anna, started a farm, and by the end of 1915, when he petitioned to become a naturalized citizen, the couple had six living children, from the eldest, Mary, born in Pennsylvania in 1905, to the youngest, Joseph, who was born on the Glendale farm on August 15, 1914.[230] When Joseph was ten, the family farm was not booming, and the Ukrops moved back to Creighton, Pennsylvania, so that Stefan could work in the steel mills. When the Depression hit, the mills closed, and they returned to Virginia and their farm.

It was Joseph who would start work with A&P and then go into the grocery business on his own, with the help of a mortgage on his father's farm. That one store would grow into the Ukrop's Super Markets chain, which for years was Richmond's leading grocer and known around the world for its innovations and customer service. The chain was sold in 2010 to Ahold, but its famous White House Rolls and prepared foods still live through Ukrop's Homestyle Foods and are sold in grocery stores up and down the East Coast.

MODEST BEGINNINGS

Joseph, who was working as a meat manager for an A&P on Grace Street, learned in 1937 that the owner of a small, less-than-eight-hundred-square-foot store, Newton's Market, in the 3000 block of Hull Street, was looking to sell. With less than $700 of inventory and a store the size of a two-car garage, he opened his doors with his wife, Jacquelin Ldevia. The store had no refrigeration, and ice was delivered every day to keep meat cold. Ukrop told reporter Steve Clark in 1987 that the value of Crisco at the end of the aisle in one of his new stores was more than what he had to offer back then.[231]

During World War II, while many farmhands were enlisted, Ukrop would close his store on Wednesdays, and he, his wife and store staff would help farmers with their crops. As he grew older, he liked picking produce from the family farm and selling it in the stores. He also figured out a way to bottle the water from a spring on the land and offer it in the stores.[232]

Above: Ukrop's Hull Street store in 1953. *Library of Virginia.*

Right: Ukrop's ad for their first two stores with Bobby Ukrop and his eventual wife. *Ukrop's Homestyle Foods, vintagerva. blogspot.com.*

Although Jane Brown needs little persuasion to buy anything from Bob Ukrop, she always buys at Ukrop's.

UKROP'S SUPER MARKETS
3111 Hull Street
6828 Midlothian Pike

Ukrop's ad listing multiple stores.
Ukrop's Homestyle Foods, vintagerva.
blogspot.com.

A second store on Midlothian didn't come along until 1963 under the urging of his son Jim, who eventually became the president of the company and grew the company with his brother Bobby to twenty-seven stores throughout central Virginia.[233]

In the 1970s, the stores were having trouble getting quality bakery products, but their dilemma was solved when they purchased Richmond-based Dot's Pastry Shop and its recipes in 1976. That pastry shop eventually became the Ukrop's Bakery, known for its cakes, pies and famous Rainbow Cookies. White House Rolls were introduced in 1984, and Ukrop's eventually opened a kitchen and bakery production facility in the 1990s to meet the growing demand for prepared foods.

In addition to high-quality products and exemplary customer service, the company still gives 10 percent of its pre-tax sales to charities combating childhood hunger and supports the Salvation Army, SportsBackers, SwimRVA and many other community groups and efforts. It also has sponsored the Monument Avenue 10k and the Dominion Christmas Parade, during which Bobby has tossed White House Rolls into the crowd.

When his father, Joe, passed away in 2002, Bobby told the *Richmond Times-Dispatch,* "He loved food. His love of food was how he communicated with people."[234]

128

THE MOVE TO LA MILPA

And that's exactly how Martin Gonzalez is picking up the grocery store mantle where Joseph Ukrop left off along Hull Street.

Gonzalez arrived in the United States from Mexico City in 1985. He opened Mexico Mini Market #1 in Henrico in 1994 and then Mexico Mini Market #2 on Jefferson Davis Highway in Chesterfield in 1997. He arrived at 6925 Hull Street Road in 2000 with La Milpa, a restaurant and market that he owns with Monica Chavez. It was also the same year Gonzalez was granted citizenship and the same year that Michel Zajur of the famed La Siesta restaurant on Midlothian Turnpike, which opened in 1972, started the Virginia Hispanic Chamber of Commerce to assist the state's growing number of Hispanic businesses.

Open twenty-four hours a day, La Milpa is a force for good food and good in the community, helping recent immigrants get a taste of home in their new country while offering traditional products for the home cook such as chorizo sausage and cheeses. Their annual Day of the Dead celebration in early November is a multi-day, multi-sensory experience with music, dancing, costumes and, of course, traditional Mexican food.[235]

On February 16, 2017, Gonzalez closed La Milpa for "A Day Without Immigrants," a social media–led campaign to demonstrate support for immigrants in light of a new presidential administration. He told the *Times-Dispatch* that he probably lost $3,000 by doing so, but it was the right thing to do.

"This is not about money," he shared with the newspaper. "It's showing I care about being part of this whole, great country."

CHAPTER 22

ROLLED THIN

Pat and Betty and Reynolds Wrap

Atrusted kitchen staple and one that is almost certainly in your kitchen had marketing materials in 1950 designed to assure consumers that it wouldn't burn their houses down: "Will aluminum foil catch fire in the oven? Can I get a shock from using aluminum foil with an electric range? Can I short circuit my range, blow the fuse, or cause other damage if aluminum foil contacts exposed wires?" Glad to know the Reynolds company line was: "The possibility is remote, since aluminum foil melts on contact."[236]

Reynolds Wrap aluminum foil might have rolled out slowly, but once the rolls were in people's homes and hands, the foil proved quite the hot product. Reynolds manufactured and test-marketed it in Richmond, including, in a bizarre twist, having demonstrators hand out samples to women shopping in the lingerie department at Thalhimers.[237] A&P purchased the first four hundred cases to supply its Virginia stores.[238] Soon the foil was being touted for everything from heating up breads in the oven to decorating one's dining table to, in the *Virginia Medical Monthly*, dressing burns![239] (Do not try this at home.)

The founder of the foil, Richard S. Reynolds, or R.S. as he was known, was born in 1881 in Bristol, Tennessee. He first worked for his uncle R.J. Reynolds in the tobacco business. The Prince Albert Tin, an all-metal container that kept tobacco fresh and dry, was the younger Reynolds's invention.[240]

Reynolds left his uncle's tobacco business to work with his brothers and, by 1919, had sold that company and started U.S. Foil, producing foils for

Trusted since 1947. An impromptu Thanksgiving experiment in Richmond helped this become a consumer classic. *Maureen Egan.*

cigarette and gum packaging. If you're of a certain vintage, you've heard people say "tin foil," which makes sense because it was made of tin (and lead). Reynolds was behind the innovation of using aluminum instead, starting in 1926. Aluminum was lighter, less expensive and had a shinier sheen, which made it a natural for consumer packaging of all sorts. In 1928, the firm became Reynolds Metal Company. After a stint in New York, it moved its headquarters in 1938 to Richmond, which already had foil plants.

A trip to Germany before World War II convinced Reynolds that Germany was buying up aluminum to prepare for war, so he returned home to warn the government and prepare his factories as well. His prescience about Germany's plans and the necessary U.S. response put the company in a position to retool factories and lease additional ones to produce aluminum for airplanes and other industrial uses. By 1942, the company could "produce 160 million pounds of virgin aluminum a year" and manufacture whatever the war effort needed.[241]

SEEING AHEAD

Even with war clouds ahead, Reynolds—who had years earlier acquired Eskimo Pie, the chocolate-covered ice cream invented in Iowa in the 1920s, since it was already making its foil wrappers—still was writing Eskimo Pie president Warren Watts in 1940 to try to boost sales in winter "and then with your artists to design an appealing wrapper, to be printed by gravure, that it will make a real hit with both the Drug and Grocery Chains who are going very fast to 'Serve Yourself' stores."

Reynolds was attuned to the changes in the grocery marketplace and wanted to capitalize on his shiny, useful product and the rotogravure printing process the company had developed: "The consumers, to our certain knowledge, are now easily switched from an old brand, in an unattractive package, to a new brand in an attractive package. Really, sales miracles are taking place right under our nose and I am ambitious for Eskimo to get in on some of this before it is too late."[242]

Even before the war was over, Reynolds was looking ahead to the next big thing. In a letter from researcher Clarence Manning to an employee: "Mr. Reynolds has referred to me your excellent idea in connection with frozen chickens. Frozen meats and food of all kinds appear to offer a big postwar field....I would not be surprised if the plain aluminum foil used in your experiment is not perhaps the answer to the wrapper."[243]

FOILED AGAIN

Manning's research on the homefront was quite literal when his wife realized on Thanksgiving Day 1944 that their turkey wouldn't fit in any roasting pan she had. She asked him to find one, but knowing it would be difficult to find on a holiday, he pulled out a roll of aluminum foil meant for research, and the day and dinner were saved. And not long thereafter, Reynolds Metals had 1,001 new uses and markets for aluminum foil.[244]

The Reynolds researchers discovered that aluminum could be rolled thin enough that one pound could cover 70,000 square inches—make a sheet five feet wide by one hundred feet long or .00017 inch thick (or thin). The foil's many advantages included its nontoxicity, the fact that it wouldn't change the taste of food it was in contact with and that it provided an impenetrable barrier to moisture, light and odors.[245]

Playful Reynolds aluminum foil newspaper ads from 1972. *Box Vox: Packaging as Content,* beachpackagingdesign.com/boxvox/reynolds-wrap-reindeer-day-8.

Once consumers got over their aforementioned skittishness, Reynolds Wrap was on a roll, and aluminum foil became ubiquitous. When the company did a foil-packaging job for FFV in the early '50s, the cookie maker tripled its sales, so then Nabisco and United Biscuit wanted foil for their products. Foil was classy.

Testing—1, 2, 3

Speaking of baking, let's turn our attention to our trusted kitchen helpers, the actual Reynolds Test Kitchen employees who once labored for Reynolds in Richmond: Betty Morton, kitchen manager, and Pat Schweitzer, senior home economist, who were featured in a long-running advertising campaign that started in 1995. The world soon knew them as Pat and Betty.

In reality, Pat and Betty were home economists working in the Reynolds Test Kitchen who tested products and recipes to use the products more effortlessly. On the television commercials, which you can still find on YouTube, they played versions of themselves as home economists in white lab coats, offering tips to save women time in the kitchen or help hapless men cook without cleanup. But as home economists, they occasionally needed a stunt double.

Producers wouldn't let Pat slide down a rope from a tree house during shooting of *Cookout Catastrophe*, so a stuntwoman did the trick for her. The early commercials were filmed in Richmond at the test kitchen, which was in the basement of the EXO building on the modernist Reynolds campus. An early commercial for the "Reynolds has it all wrapped up" campaign put Pat in a parka in a nonfunctioning walk-in freezer made to look freezing with dry ice. The steamy set-up made Pat so hot that a producer bought her a fan and put it up her shirt in between takes. It soon became clear that filming the commercials in the test kitchen interfered with ongoing work there, so, as Pat remembered, they "filmed in New York, Orlando, Los Angeles and Toronto, including in George Clooney's neighborhood one time." They may not have met Clooney, but they did meet Julia Child and Marcus Samuelsson in their travels, according to Betty.

They became celebrities and had their own book, *Pat & Betty's No-Fuss Cooking.* In 1997, the duo embarked on a rock star tour in a custom mobile kitchen to perform demos, meet their fans and celebrate the fiftieth anniversary of Reynolds Wrap. They were instrumental in popularizing the foil-packet cooking trend and no-mess grilling. Betty is especially proud that the "Reynolds Kitchens team developed many Vegetable Packet recipes that encourage us to eat more colorful, nutritious vegetables."

Their almost ten-year run as celebrities came to an official end in 2006, though they still made appearances and worked for Alcoa, which bought Reynolds Metals that year. Foil production moved to Louisville, and after several years, the north plant in Shockoe Slip was redeveloped into apartments, a restaurant and offices.

Betty lives in North Carolina now and provides food coaching on healthy eating through her company, Betty's Good Cooking, and occasionally teaches healthy cooking classes in Winston-Salem. She's working on a cookbook, too. All this while she says she's happily retired! And even though Pat is now manager of the Hamilton Beach Consumer Test Kitchen (also in Richmond), she still says, "For cooking turkeys, I am a big fan of the Reynolds Oven Bag. It cooks the turkey quicker and keeps it moist and juicy."

As homage to Reynolds Wrap's history in Richmond, wrap a chicken and some veggies in foil for dinner and have an Eskimo Pie for dessert.

CHAPTER 23

"CAN'T EAT...DON'T BUY"

Lunch Counter Sit-Ins

O n November 1, 2014, in Richmond at the Library of Virginia—fifty years after the passage of the Civil Rights Act of 1964 that mandated customers of all races be served in all public places throughout the country—two Richmonders came to the table to discuss their families' roles in that ruling.[246] Though they sat at opposite ends of the table, they were united in spirit.

On the left was the granddaughter of a Jewish merchant whose store's restaurant, the Richmond Room, and lunch counters weren't integrated in 1960, nor were its bathrooms and dressing rooms—despite having black employees, black customers and an integrated employee cafeteria.[247]

Behind the table on the far right was an African American woman who came to the Thalhimers lunch counter on Monday, February 22, 1960, and subsequently was one of thirty-four arrested, rounded up by police and charged with trespassing—cited as one of the largest mass arrests of the civil rights movement at the time.[248]

The two women, Elizabeth Thalhimer Smartt and Elizabeth Johnson-Rice, met for the first time after a 2004 sit-in remembrance ceremony, held in front of the old Thalhimers store, which had closed in January 1992, 150 years after its founding in 1842.

Not knowing if any Thalhimer family members would show up, Johnson-Rice had plaques ready. She handed Smartt engraved plaques for her grandfather William B. Thalhimer Jr. and her great-uncle Charles G. Thalhimer Sr. "Good gracious," Johnson-Rice said. "I'm so glad you

DON'T BUY AT WOOLWORTH

In many southern states—students—both Negro and white—are sitting in at lunch counters, quietly but persistently demanding that Woolworth serve everyone—regardless of color.

THESE STUDENTS FACE:
Mass arrests . . . Exorbitant fines . . . Threats of expulsion from school. In some cases, they sit while segregationist hoodlums brandish knives, hammers and baseball bats. Yet,

WOOLWORTH CAN SERVE:
Discriminatory seating in most cases is *NOT* required by law. Even where such laws exist, they are obviously unconstitutional. In a matter of minutes, Woolworth management in New York City can direct its southern stores to serve everyone.

YOU CAN MAKE WOOLWORTH SERVE:
This and every other Woolworth store is directly controlled by the national chain. Every dime and dollar spent here is an open endorsement of the chain's policy of racial segregation and discrimination. *DON'T BACK* the knives and hammers of segregationist hoodlums *WITH YOUR MONEY*.

DON'T BUY AT WOOLWORTH
JOIN CORE'S PICKET LINES. Ask all other men of goodwill not to shop jimcrow.

CORE   Congress of Racial Equality
38 Park Row, New York 38, New York
COrtlandt 7-0408

Congress of Racial Equality's anti-Woolworth campaign. 1962: 62004-00652 c.1: Broadsides, *Virginia Historical Society.*

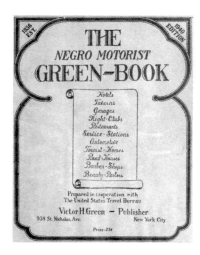

The 1940 *Negro Motorist Green-Book. New York Public Library.*

[came]. I hope you'll convey to your family how much we appreciate what they did."[249]

By January 1, 1961, Thalhimers had integrated all its facilities, but let's go back to the beginning of 1960.

On February 1, 1960, four college students in Greensboro, North Carolina, entered a Woolworth's, purchased toothpaste and then asked for coffee at the lunch counter but were denied service. Their action began a national lunch counter sit-in movement against racial segregation in public but privately owned places—a movement that would spread across the South.[250] The specific legal question centered on whether the Fourteenth Amendment, which after *Brown v. Board of Education* prohibited racial segregation in schools and other state-operated facilities, applied to privately owned accommodations open to the general public.[251]

In the 1940s and 1950s, many African Americans usually traveled with the *Negro Motorist Green-Book*, a directory that listed the hotels, dining establishments and service stations that would accommodate them. In Richmond, for instance, the Eggleston Hotel at Second and Leigh Streets in Jackson Ward, the epicenter of black entrepreneurism, was listed.[252]

In early February 1960, Virginia Union University students began preparing for their sit-ins—nonviolent direct action, as inspired by the Reverend Martin Luther King Jr., who had spoken on their campus the year before. The students practiced demonstrating; lined up legal counsel, including civil rights lawyer Oliver Hill;

and visited black churches on Sunday, February 14, explaining their protest and seeking congregational support—picketing and boycotting stores, if necessary.[253]

"We didn't know what to expect," Johnson-Rice's brother Ford Johnson Jr. told *Richmond* magazine in 2010. He was eighteen and a sophomore chemistry major. "We'd all seen the pictures everyone else had seen, the water hoses, the beatings, the whole deal. Here we were in Richmond, the cradle of the Confederacy, where nothing like this had been tried."[254]

Some two hundred students marched downtown on Saturday, February 20. They sat at all the department store and drugstore counters between Fourth and Sixth Streets but were not served. Those establishments included Thalhimers, Woolworth's, Murphy's and People's Service Drug Store.

Woolworth's closed the counter to customers after thirty-four Virginia Union students sat down. At 9:30 a.m., Murphy's closed its counter after seventy-four students took seats there. Both stores had closed completely by 1:00 p.m. Students then walked to Thalhimers and sat at the soda fountain near the Sixth Street entrance. The store remained open, but the store's restaurants were closed for the rest of the day. No one was arrested.

Picketing along Broad Street, February 1960. *The Anderson Collection, The Valentine.*

A protest at Thalhimers' Richmond Room, February 1960. *The Anderson Collection, The Valentine.*

Lunch counter sit-ins in stores along Broad Street downtown. *The Richard Anderson Collection, Albert and Shirley Small Special Collections Library, the University of Virginia.*

On Monday, February 22, five hundred students walked downtown from their Lombardy Street campus. The Woolworth's counter was closed, as was Murphy's.

Johnson-Rice, then a nineteen-year-old junior at Virginia Union, active in both the Student Nonviolent Coordinating Committee and the Southern Christian Leadership Conference, joined her brother Ford and the other students marching to Thalhimers.[255] "I used to love to go into Thalhimers," she recalled in a 2006 *Richmond Times-Dispatch* article. "I remember the smell of the bakery. The negative thing I remember is…At the lunch counter, I couldn't eat there."

Johnson-Rice and her brother joined the group sitting at the first-floor lunch counter. Others went upstairs to the Richmond Room. The students were taunted, and Johnson-Rice said someone dropped hot coffee in her lap.[256]

Police officers and police dogs soon entered the store. The police told them, "You can all leave now, or you can be arrested." No one left the counter.

The students were taken to jail and released after the NAACP and others posted bail for them. They then gathered at Neverett A. Eggleston Sr.'s hotel in Jackson Ward, where parents and school administrators were waiting for them. It was "Nat" Eggleston who also encouraged other black-owned businesses to support the students.[257] "We got to the Eggleston Hotel, and all these people were there," Johnson-Rice said. "I look out and see my mother and father in the crowd. And instead of being angry at us, my father was very proud."[258]

"I think everyone was just glad to see we still had our heads," her brother added.[259]

The sit-ins were followed by boycotts and picketing of segregated retail establishments. "The theme was: Don't buy where you could be arrested or where you can't eat. Pressure built by Christmastime, and one by one, the stores gave up their racial policies. Make no bones about it, this ignited the end of segregation here," said VUU history professor Raymond P. Hylton.[260]

In November 1960, shortly after Thanksgiving, William B. Thalhimer Jr. met with heads of the black community in the Richmond Room, and Web Rhoads Jr. invited other black leaders to have dinner with him in the Miller & Rhoads Tea Room.

"That was the beginning of us quietly integrating our restaurants," Thalhimer Jr. said. By January 1, 1961, Thalhimers' public and private spaces were open to all.[261]

Miller's Hotel, which became the Eggleston Hotel in Jackson Ward. *Library of Congress.*

But it wasn't until June 10, 1963, that the U.S. Supreme Court threw out the trespassing convictions of the "Richmond 34" as a violation of the U.S. Constitution's equal protection clause under the Fourteenth Amendment.

In early summer, according to an August 26, 1963 *Richmond News Leader* story, thirty-five Richmond restaurants voluntarily desegregated after a climactic day of negotiations with civil rights leaders. Previously, an estimated twenty-five had desegregated and another ten were in the process, said E.L. Slade Jr., president of the Richmond NAACP. The local NAACP youth council and its VUU affiliate had been focusing their efforts on restaurants.[262] A *Times-Dispatch* headline on August 3, 1963, read, "Restaurants Here See Little Effect from Integration."[263]

Despite its June 10 ruling in favor of the Richmond 34, the Supreme Court still limited congressional enforcement of the Fourteenth Amendment to state actions, rather than individual actions. To remedy that, Congress, with its purview to regulate interstate commerce, passed the Civil Rights Act of 1964, which prohibited discrimination based on religion, race or origin in public establishments that were connected by interstate commerce or were supported by the state. Hotels, restaurants, gas stations and other entertainment venues were included.[264]

The *Negro Motorist Green-Book* ceased publication in 1964, nearly thirty years after it began.

In July 2016, a historical marker dedicated to the Richmond 34 went up on Broad Street near the old Thalhimers store site. Elizabeth Johnson-Rice, Ford Johnson Jr. and Elizabeth Thalhimer Smartt all attended.

Thalhimers' famous six-layer cake and other baked goods are being made at Michaela's Quality Bake Shop in Brookland Park by former Thalhimer baker Michael Hatcher.

CHAPTER 24

THE RECIPE BOX

A Collection of Old and New Favorites

Within this chapter are some recipes from historical resources that have not been tested. Makers and bakers, beware.

POWHATAN SQUASH AND CORN SOUP

Adapted by K. Lara Templin, Jamestown-Yorktown Foundation

¼ cup butter (or 3–4 tablespoons nut oil like hazelnut oil if you want vegan
and don't worry about nut allergies)
Scant teaspoon of salt
½ teaspoon ground hot red pepper (cayenne or similar)*
I butternut squash, peeled and cubed*
2 cups cooked pumpkin mush*
I cup dried sweet corn*
3 cups water

Put the butter or oil in the soup pot and add the salt and red pepper, then the squash and stir it around a few minutes. Then add the pumpkin and dried corn and stir a few minutes. Finally, add the water and cook on low, stirring occasionally, at least an hour (or slow cook 4 hours). If the squash is not completely falling apart into mush, use an immersion blender for a minute or two until a relatively smooth texture is achieved. The soup should be thick and rich.

Notes:

Go lighter on the red pepper if you think it is too spicy; I think it is mild, but I like spice!

You can use a 20-ounce package of frozen butternut squash cubes.

You can use 1 15- to 16-ounce can of pumpkin—not one already spiced for pie!

Do NOT use fresh or frozen corn. John Cope's toasted dried sweet corn works.

PICKLED STURGEON

From William Byrd's Diaries, *Vol. 2*
"Mr Catesby's Receipt to Pickle Sturgeon"

To pickle Sturgeon*

Let the fish when taken cool on the ground 24, 36 or 48 hours as the Weather will permit, then cut it in pieces, & throw it into clean Water, shifting the Water several times, whilst it is soaking wash and brush it with hard Brushes til it be very clean, which it will be in two or three Hours, And then you may tie it up with Bass and Boyl it; Put in Somewhat more Salt than in boiling other Fish, Skim it well and boil it very softly, til it be tender, an hour, or an hour and a half or 2 hours according to the Age of the Fish. And then let it cool very well, And put it into pickle. The Pickle must be made of Beer Vinegar ⅝ & ⅜ of the Broth it was boiled and mixed together & Salt the Pickle very well with unbeat Salt somewhat more than will make a fresh Egg swim, put the Fish in the Kettle when the water is cold and the Fat must be taken off very well.

*It is illegal to catch wild sturgeon in the United States. Farmed sturgeon is available from Atlantic Caviar and Sturgeon.

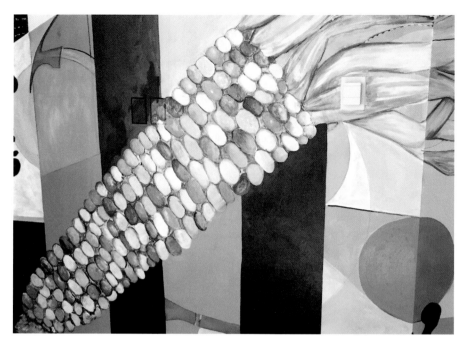

Richmond artist Diego Sanchez's mural spices up the VMFA's Art Education Center. *Susan Winiecki.*

MRS. PATRICK HENRY'S POUND CAKE

Mrs. Patrick Henry most assuredly did not have easy access to lemon and vanilla extracts, but thanks to C.F. Sauer Company, you do. This recipe is from Byrd Mill Since 1740, Louisa, Virginia: 18th Century Virginia Receipts *and was once used in Williamsburg's Raleigh Bakeshop (from the Virginia Historical Society's general collection).*

1 Cup Butter
1½ Cups Sugar
2⅓ Cups natural flour
5 Eggs
½ Cup Milk
1 Teaspoon each Lemon and Vanilla Extract

Cream Butter until it can be beaten with a Spoon before adding Sugar. Add Sugar gradually, beating Mixture until creamy. Separate Eggs, beat Yolks until thick and Whites until Stiff. Add beaten Yolks to Butter and

Sugar; mix well, then add a Portion of Flour, stir until smooth, then fold in Portion of Milk, continue to stir in Flour and Milk alternately mixing until smooth. Add Flavoring and Egg Whites. Pour into an ungreased Paper-lined Pan. Bake in a slow Oven (325) 1 Hour for a square or round Pan, longer than one Hour if oblong Pan is used. Cool thoroughly before cutting.

QUOIT CLUB PUNCH

This recipe for Quoit Club Punch comes from Thomas Leggett, bar manager at The Roosevelt, adapted from Dave Wondrich's indispensable book, Punch. *The Roosevelt and T, as he is known, won Elbys in 2013 and 2017 for Best Cocktail Program.*
Makes just shy of a gallon

Start by combining the peels of 12 lemons and 2 cups of sugar in a bowl. Muddle the mixture lightly and let stand for 1 hour. This process will extract the aromatic oils from the lemon peels to give depth to the punch. Afterward add 2 cups of fresh, strained lemon juice and stir until sugar is dissolved. Add a 750 ml bottle of good Jamaican rum, another of a good aged brandy and finally a 750 ml bottle of rainwater Madeira. Stir until well integrated and add to a punch bowl filled with plenty of ice; larger blocks preferred for longevity of the social engagement.

GASPACHA—SPANISH

See chapter 6 for background on this recipe from Mary Randolph's 1824 cookbook.

Put some soft biscuit or toasted bread in the bottom of a sallad bowl, put in a layer of sliced tomatos with the skin taken off, and one of sliced cucumbers, sprinkled with pepper, salt and chopped onion; do this until the bowl is full; stew some tomatos quite soft, strain the juice, mix in some mustard, oil, and water, and pour over it; make it two hours before it is eaten.

MRS. HORACE W. JONES' LOAF BREAD, ROLLS AND TURNOVERS

From Virginia Cookery Book, *compiled by the Virginia League of Women Voters in 1921*
This recipe moved through several bakers' hands to possibly become the rolls served at
Morton's Tea Room. Perhaps the recipe's vagueness on some scores, as in temperature and
time, is meant to ensure that no one will ever make her famous rolls as well as her cooks
did, but give it a try. "Quick oven" means hot oven, if that helps!

½ yeast cake (for quick bread in cold weather use 2 cakes)
1 teaspoon salt
1 quart flour
1 tablespoon lard
3 teaspoons sugar
1 pint liquid

Dissolve yeast cake in lukewarm water. Sift salt and flour together. Make a hole in middle of flour. Put in lard, sugar and dissolved yeast cake. Add water by degrees, while mixing dough. Knead until perfectly smooth, grease top and put in greased crock in warm place. It is very necessary for good bread to keep the dough at an even temperature. Rise until it has doubled its bulk (70 degrees is a good temperature). Put down in any shape preferred. When this has doubled its bulk, bake in quick oven. The last few minutes the heat should be lowered.

SALLY BELL'S KITCHEN HAM SPREAD

Sally Bell's used to get its Virginia hams from J.P. Crowder's in Jackson Ward. You didn't
expect them to give away their potato salad recipe, did you?!
Makes 18 sandwiches

2 pounds ground picnic shoulder ham
2 cups seedless raisins, ground
1 8-ounce package cream cheese, softened
¾ cup mayonnaise
⅔ cup sweet relish

In a medium bowl, mix ham and raisins thoroughly. Blend in cream cheese and mayonnaise. Stir in relish.

Downtown Richmond when Sixth Street Market and its environs were bustling. *Library of Virginia.*

Thalhimers' Soup Bar Pimento Cheese

Recipe from Louis Mahoney's "Thalhimers' Signature Dishes Won't Be Signing Out" in the Richmond Times-Dispatch, January 15, 1992

Thalhimers in Richmond had a Men's Soup Bar on the mezzanine level for many years, ostensibly where businessmen could grab a quick lunch away from the more leisurely ladies. Eight women walked in to be served in 1970 and were at first refused. One man was quoted as saying, "There goes the last place to eat in town!"

Makes about 6 cups

¼ cup margarine
½ cup flour
1 pound sharp cheddar cheese, shredded
1 large green bell pepper, finely diced
½ cup chopped pimento

In a saucepan over medium heat, melt margarine. Stirring constantly to keep from lumping, sprinkle flour over. Continue stirring and cook until slightly thickened and pale golden. Remove from heat.

Place cheese, bell pepper and pimento in a large bowl. Stir in flour mixture until completely blended. Chill thoroughly before serving.

The days of Richmond-made flour have washed away with the tide, unless you go to Sub Rosa! These factories and mills are on the Manchester side of the James, 1865. *Library of Congress.*

MILLER & RHOADS CHOCOLATE PIE

Thanks to our friends at the Hilton Richmond Downtown for this sweet taste of the past, also known as Chocolate Silk Pie. A Miller & Rhoads display inside the hotel is worth a trip down memory lane.
Serves 8/Prep Time: 35 minutes/Total Time: 40 minutes

Crust
½ cup butter
½ cup granulated sugar
2 cups graham cracker crumbs

Filling
½ cup unsalted butter
¾ cup confectioners' sugar
1 ounce unsweetened baking chocolate, melted and cooled
1 pinch salt
1 teaspoon vanilla extract
3 eggs* (or pasteurized liquid eggs)

Garnish
2 cups sweetened whipped cream
chocolate sprinkles or shaved semisweet chocolate

Crust: Preheat oven to 350 degrees. Beat butter and granulated sugar with an electric mixer until light and fluffy. Gradually mix in just enough crumbs to make a slightly crumbly paste. Press evenly into a chilled 8-inch pie plate. Bake 5 minutes. Cool to room temperature.

Filling: With an electric mixer, beat butter and confectioners' sugar until light and fluffy. Add melted chocolate with salt and vanilla. Add 1 egg and beat for no less than 5 additional minutes. Add second egg and beat no less than 3 minutes. Add third egg and beat no less than 5 minutes longer. Pour filling into prepared shell and refrigerate for 24 hours.

Garnish: Just before serving, decorate top of pie with sweetened whipped cream and sprinkle with chocolate.

Note: Do not try to rush this recipe. Beating each egg separately for no less than 5 minutes each is the secret. #OHMYPIE
*Uncooked eggs can contain salmonella, which can cause severe illness, particularly among infants, the elderly and those with compromised immune systems. If you are concerned about the quality of the eggs you are using, substitute with pasteurized liquid eggs.

The Best Devil's Food Cake with Salted Caramel Buttercream

By Jessica Aber, Richmond, Virginia
This cake won the devil's food cake contest at the 2015 FFF Urban State Fair, part of Fire,
Flour & Fork. The contest was presented by C.F. Sauer, and judges included members of
the Advanced Food Service Training Division at Fort Lee, Erin Hatcher of C.F. Sauer and
Beth Royals, Richmond's own Pillsbury Bake-Off Champion. It won forks down!

Cake

1 cup hot coffee
4 ounces bittersweet chocolate, chopped (¾ cup)
2 cups King Arthur unbleached all-purpose flour
1 teaspoon salt
1 teaspoon baking powder
2 teaspoons baking soda
¾ cup unsweetened cocoa powder
1 cup white sugar
¾ cup brown sugar
1 cup Duke's Mayonnaise
1 cup buttermilk
2 large eggs
1 teaspoon Sauer's pure vanilla extract

Preheat oven to 325°F. Butter two 9-inch round cake pans. Line bottoms with parchment rounds; butter parchment.

Stir together hot coffee and bittersweet chocolate in a bowl until chocolate melts.

In a separate mixing bowl, stir together dry ingredients.

Add mayonnaise, buttermilk and coffee and chocolate mixture to dry ingredients. Using an electric mixer, beat at medium speed for 2 minutes. Add eggs and vanilla and beat 2 more minutes.

Pour into cake pans. Bake at 325°F for about 30 minutes, or until a toothpick inserted in the center comes out clean. Cool in pans for about 15 minutes and then cool completely on racks.

Frost cakes with salted caramel buttercream.

Salted Caramel Buttercream Frosting

12 tablespoons butter, softened
4 ounces Neufchatel (low-fat cream cheese)
½ cup Duke's Mayonnaise

1 cup dulce de leche
2 teaspoons Sauer's pure vanilla extract
1 ½ teaspoons coarse sea salt
4 cups confectioners' sugar

Using an electric mixer, beat butter on medium speed until creamy.

Add Neufchatel, mayonnaise, dulce de leche, vanilla and salt. Beat until fully incorporated, scraping down the sides of the bowl as necessary with a rubber spatula.

Gradually add 4 cups of confectioners' sugar, beating on low speed, until well combined. Beat on high speed until well combined and smooth while scraping down sides of the bowl as necessary, about 2 minutes.

DUKE'S CHOCOLATE CAKE

Duke's Mayonnaise famously has no sugar in it, which makes it about the only mayonnaise you'll want to put in a chocolate cake recipe. Duke's celebrated its 100th birthday in April 2017. This cake recipe, from the folks at Duke's (part of C.F. Sauer), will make anyone's birthday memorable.

Cake
6 tablespoons unsweetened cocoa
3 cups all-purpose flour
1 tablespoon baking soda
¼ teaspoon salt
1 ½ cups sugar
1 ½ cups Duke's Mayonnaise
1 ½ teaspoons Sauer's Vanilla Extract
1 ½ cups cold water

Chocolate Icing
1 cup butter, softened
1 cup cocoa
1 teaspoon vanilla extract
5–6 cups confectioners' sugar
6 or more tablespoons milk

Preheat oven to 350°F, grease and flour two 8-inch cake pans. Sift cocoa, flour, baking soda, salt and sugar into a medium bowl; mix well. Combine mayonnaise, vanilla and water in an electric mixer at low speed. Once smooth, slowly add in dry mixture until just incorporated (do not overbeat). Pour batter into cake pans and bake for 30 minutes or until done. Cool on wire racks and frost. For the frosting, in the bowl of an electric mixer, beat butter and cocoa with whisk attachment until smooth. Add vanilla. Add confectioners' sugar alternately with milk until icing reaches a spreadable consistency. Note: you may not need all 6 cups of sugar; you may need more than 6 tablespoons of milk.

CHARLOTTE'S GREEN TRANSFORMATION SALAD DRESSING

From Charlotte Kenhey, a cook at Grace Place, the beloved and long-gone all-vegetarian place on Grace Street.

2 cups safflower oil
3 full leaves any green leafy vegetable: kale, spinach or lettuce
3 sprigs parsley
4 cloves garlic
½ large onion
¼ cup tamari sauce or soy
½ lemon, rind and juice
½ cup apple juice
¼ cup vinegar

Place all ingredients in blender and blend until well mixed. Add basil or thyme to taste.

MAMA J'S SWEET POTATO PIE

Velma Johnson started a career as a caterer as she ended her career in the Richmond Sheriff's Department. Her experience helping prepare meals as one of fourteen children growing up contributed to her ease of cooking for crowds. The space on North First Street was too perfect for a restaurant to pass up, so now the crowds flock to Mama J's to taste the home-like cooking.
Makes 4 pies.

6 cups mashed sweet potatoes
6 eggs
2 teaspoons nutmeg
1 teaspoon cinnamon
1 teaspoon lemon extract
2 cups sugar
1 package instant lemon pudding
pinch salt
1 ½ cups milk

Mix all. Fill 4 medium uncooked pie shells. Cook slowly at 300°F for 2 hours.

NOTES

Chapter 1

1. Manarin and Dowdey, *History of Henrico County*.
2. Joe Heim, "A Renowned Virginia Indian Tribe Finally Wins Federal Recognition," *Washington Post*, July 2, 2015.
3. Tyler, *Narratives of Early Virginia*, 33.
4. Rountree, *Powhatan Indians of Virginia*, 47, 50.
5. Tyler, *Narratives of Early Virginia*, 18.
6. Ibid.
7. Rountree, *Powhatan Indians of Virginia*, 34.
8. Ibid., 34, 50.
9. Tyler, *Narratives of Early Virginia*, 97.
10. Rountree, *Powhatan Indians of Virginia*, 39–40.
11. Ibid., 51.
12. Historic Richmond Foundation, *Richmond's Historic Waterfront*, 5.
13. Virginia Foundation for the Humanities, "Encounter: The Mattaponi River," www.virginiaindianarchive.org/items/show/123, May 2007.

Chapter 2

14. Michael Demarest, "He Digs Downtown," *Time*, August 24, 1981, 46.
15. Ibid., 53; Bloom, *Merchant of Illusion*, 92.

16. Shelley Rolfe, "A Bridge to the Past," *Richmond Times-Dispatch*, September 29, 1984.
17. Ibid.
18. Gibson Worsham and Richard Worsham, "Richmond's Second and Third Markets," urbanscalerichmondvirginia.blogspot.com, December 2012.
19. Elizabeth Dabney Coleman, "Richmond's Flowering Second Market," *Virginia Cavalcade* 4, no. 4 (Spring 1955): 10.
20. *Richmond Times-Dispatch*, "Cooks Page," February 17, 1922, 5.
21. Worsham and Worsham, "Richmond's Second and Third Markets."
22. Jeanne Cummings, "Marketplace Opens Amid Great Fanfare," *Richmond News Leader*, September 18, 1985.
23. Carol O'Connor Wolf, "It's Opening! Sixth Street Marketplace," *Style Weekly*, September 10, 1985.
24. Rob Walker, "Spent Enough, Rouse Says," *Richmond Times-Dispatch*, February 22, 1988.
25. "Norfolk Firm Hired Again to Run 6th St. Marketplace," *Richmond Free Press*, April 18, 1996, 5.

Chapter 3

26. Potterfield, *Nonesuch Place*, 29.
27. Historic Richmond Foundation, *Richmond's Historic Waterfront*, 11.
28. Thomas Berry, "Rise of Flour Milling in Richmond," *VA Magazine*, October 1970, 393, 397.
29. Raber Associates, Historical and Archaeological Assessment of Tredegar Iron Works Site, prepared for Valentine Museum and Ethyl Corporation, 42, Lyle Browning Collection.
30. Berry, "Rise of Flour Milling in Richmond," 388–89.
31. Ibid., 406.
32. Ibid., 387.
33. *Richmond News Leader*, October 5, 1940.
34. Elizabeth Callahan Myrtle, "History of Richmond as a Port City," master's thesis, University of Richmond, June 1952.

Chapter 4

35. Karl Blankenship, "VA Scientists Searching for Secrets of Stealthy Sturgeon," *Bay Journal*, June 1, 2007.

36. Berland, *Dividing Line Histories of William Byrd II*, 213.

37. Beverly, *History and Present State of Virginia*, 113.

38. Smith, *Journals of Capt. John Smith*, 146.

39. Woodlief, *In River Time*, 57.

40. Charles Washington Coleman, "Sturgeon Fishing in the James," *Cosmopolitan*, May–October 1892, 366.

41. *Richmond Dispatch*, September 25, 1856, 1.

42. Woodlief, *In River Time*, 58.

43. Blankenship, "VA Scientists Searching for Secrets of Stealthy Sturgeon."

44. Coleman, "Sturgeon Fishing in the James," 370.

Chapter 5

45. Dabney, *Richmond*, 69.

46. Edmund Berkeley Jr., "Quoits: The Sport of Gentlemen," *Virginia Cavalcade* (Summer 1965): 11–21.

47. Munford, *Two Parsons*, 333.

48. Berkeley, "Quoits."

49. Richmond Light Infantry Blues Scrapbook, Library of Virginia Special Collections.

50. Munford, *Two Parsons*, 331.

51. Letter from Colonel Ellis, Virginia Historical Society.

52. Munford, *Two Parsons*, 331.

53. Sallie E. Marshall Hardy, "John Marshall," *The Green Bag*, December 1896.

54. Berkeley, "Quoits."

Chapter 6

55. Jose Andres, "Jose Andres: What It Means to Cook American Food," theplate.nationalgeographic.com, July 24, 2014.

56. Miller, *Soul Food*, 115.

57. Margaret Husted, "Mary Randolph's *The Virginia Housewife*: America's First Regional Cookbook," *Virginia Cavalcade* (Autumn 1980): 77–87.

58. Sterling Anderson, "Queen Molly and *The Virginia Housewife*," *Virginia Cavalcade* (Spring 1971): 28–35.

59. Ibid., 34.

60. Mordecai, *Richmond in By-Gone Days*, 129.

61. Ibid., 130.

62. 1810 U.S. Census

63. Randolph, *Virginia House-wife*, with historical notes and commentaries by Karen Hess, xxi.

64. Ibid., xxxix.

65. Husted, "Mary Randolph's *The Virginia Housewife*," 83.

66. Russell, *Domestic Cookbook*.

67. Ray Schreiner, "The First Southern Cookbook Was Penned by Richmonder Mary Randolph," *Fifty Plus*, September 1991, 8.

Chapter 7

68. Valentine Museum, "Richmond Portraits in an Exhibition of Makers of Richmond, 1737–1860," 1949, 148.

69. Kliman, *Wild Vine*, 12.

70. Dabney, *Richmond*, 137.

71. Clifford P. and Rebecca K.R. Ambers, "Dr. Daniel Norborne Norton and the Origin of the Norton Grape," *American Wine Society Journal* 36, no. 3 (Fall 2004).

72. Fuller, *Grape Culturist*, 227–28.

73. www.virginiawine.org; www.missourwinecountry.com.

74. Hylton, *Dishing Up Virginia*, 109.

75. Gabriella Lacombe, "The History of Norton," *RVAmag.com*, March 29, 2017.

Chapter 8

76. McGraw, *At the Falls*.

77. Kierner, Loux and Shockley, *Changing History*, 155–56.

78. McGraw, *At the Falls*.

79. Varon, *Southern Lady*.

80. Michael Chesson, "Harlots or Heroines?: A New Look at the Richmond Bread Riot," *Virginia Magazine of History and Biography* 92, no. 2 (April 1984): 135.
81. Ibid., 134.
82. Ibid., 139, 144.
83. Ibid., 144–45.
84. Ibid., 147–48.
85. McGraw, *At the Falls.*
86. Chesson, "Harlots or Heroines," 161.

Chapter 9

87. Wendell P. Dabney Papers, 1904–1964, n.d., Mss qD115, Cincinnati Museum Center, autobiographical sketch, 68.
88. Philip J. Schwarz, "John Dabney (ca. 1824–1900)," Encyclopedia Virginia, December 11, 2013, www.encyclopediavirginia.org/Dabney_John_ca_1824-1900.
89. Wendell P. Dabney Papers, 47.
90. John Mitchell, "Thomas Page Nelson's Conclusions," *Richmond Planet*, December 31, 1904, 4.
91. Wendell Dabney, "Why John Dabney Finished Paying for Self after the War," *Richmond Planet*, May 28, 1938.
92. Jane Taylor Duke, "Confederate Veteran Recalls Famous Negro Caterer," *Richmond News Leader*, April 15, 1938.
93. Robert Moss, "The Nat Fuller Feast Opens a New Chapter in Charleston's Forgotten Culinary History," *Charleston City Paper*, April 2015.
94. Kimball, *American City, Southern Place*, 43; Maurie D. McInnis, "Eyre Crowe's Images of the Slave Trade," Encyclopedia Virginia, April 10, 2013, www.encyclopediavirginia.org/Slave_Trade_Eyre_Crowe_s_Images_of_the#start_entry.
95. Dabney, "Why John Dabney Finished Paying for Self After the War"; Dabney Papers, 24.
96. Noted transfers from Richmond City Hustings Court Deed Books within the Encyclopedia Virginia research folder on John Dabney at Library of Virginia and city directories.
97. Dabney Papers, 24; Duke, "Confederate Veteran Recalls Famous Negro Caterer."
98. Dabney Papers, 35.

99. *Daily Dispatch*, November 20, 1862, found on mdgorman.com.

100. Dabney Papers, 37.

101. Duke, "Confederate Veteran Recalls Famous Negro Caterer."

102. *Times*, "John Dabney Dead," June 8, 1900, 7; *Richmond Dispatch*, "The Well Known Colored Caterer Dies After Two Weeks Illness," n.d., 2.

103. *Pittsburgh Courier*, "Mrs. Fannie Robinson Weds John M. Dabney Jr.," April 27, 1946.

Chapter 10

104. Alexander, *Virginia*, 108.

105. *Richmond Times-Dispatch*, "Richmond Women Outside the Home," June 3, 1927.

106. *Richmond Times-Dispatch*, "Pickles Put Richmond on Business Map," October 11, 1925.

107. M.T. Montsinger, "Where There's a Will There's a Way," Essex County Historical Society newsletter 40 (April 1994): 1.

108. *Richmond Times-Dispatch*, ad, "The Phenomenal Growth of an Unusual Enterprise," March 20, 1910.

109. Schreiner, *Women Entrepreneurs of Richmond*, 6.

110. Alexander, *Virginia*, 108; *Richmond Times-Dispatch*, "Charters Issued," August 2, 1913, 2; *Richmond Times-Dispatch*, "New Members," October 14, 1913, 2.

111. Larry Hall, "Pin Money Pickles Turned Women's Skill into Empire, *Richmond Times-Dispatch*, August 3, 2005.

112. Alexander, *Virginia*, 107.

113. Hall, "Pin Money Pickles."

Chapter 11

114. C.F. Sauer Sr., "Autobiography," October 8, 1918.

115. Ibid.

116. C.F. Sauer & Co., *Sauer's*.

117. *Greenville News*, October 1957.

118. C.F. Sauer & Co., *Sauer's*.

119. *Greenville News*, October 1957.

120. Ibid.

121. Ibid.

Chapter 12

122. *Virginia* 74, no. 2, "Valentine's Meat-Juice Serving Millions" (February 1952): 12–16.
123. Valentine Meat Juice pamphlet, Valentine Archives.
124. Ibid.
125. Ibid.
126. *Rochester Democrat and Chronicle*, "Convalescence Near," July 16, 1881.
127. *Richmond Times*, "Valentine Company Wins," August 4, 1900.
128. *Richmond Times*, "The Way to Kill Beef," May 15, 1895.
129. *New York Times*, "A Clan Called Valentine Gathers for the First Time," February 13, 1983.

Chapter 13

130. Ray Schreiner, *Big Business in Richmond: The T.W. Wood & Sons Story*, 2010.
131. T.W. Wood & Sons, "T.W. Wood Catalog," 1893.
132. Timothy Ward Wood II, "Westmoreland Place," (manuscript) collection of Virginia Historical Society, 1993.
133. Tyler, *Men of Mark*.
134. Wood, "Westmoreland Place."
135. Southern Foodways Alliance, "SFA Honors Ira Wallace," October 3, 2016, www.southernfoodways.org/sfa-honors-ira-wallace.

Chapter 14

136. *Richmond Dispatch*, "Mr. Ginter Receives," February 10, 1892.
137. Emily J. Salmon, "Belle of the Nineties: Richmond's Jefferson Hotel, 1895–1995," *Virginia Cavalcade* 45 (Summer 1995): 4.
138. Ibid., 6.
139. *Richmond Dispatch*, October 27, 1895.
140. Salmon, "Belle of the Nineties," 7.
141. Jefferson Hotel files, Virginia Historical Society.
142. *Richmond Times Dispatch*, April 26, 1903.
143. Harry Kollatz Jr., "Boundary Crashers," *Richmond* magazine, April 9, 2014.
144. *Washington Post*, "Thomas Jefferson Would Have Slept Here," August 17, 1986.

Chapter 15

145. McGraw, *At the Falls*.
146. Meacham, *Every Home a Distillery*, 12.
147. Megan Gambino, "During Prohibition, Your Doctor Could Write You a Prescription Booze," Smithsonian.com, October 7, 2013, www.smithsonianmag.com/history/during-prohibition-your-doctor-could-write-you-prescription-booze-180947940.
148. Dabney, *Richmond*, 315.
149. Ibid.
150. *New York Times*, "Richmond, VA Raid," August 11, 1930.
151. Dabney, *Richmond*.
152. Grant Martin, "Byrd Park's Temperance Fountain," RVANews.com, February 23, 2015.

Chapter 16

153. Alison Griffin, *Richmond Times Dispatch*, September 12, 1976.
154. Richmond Exchange for Women's Work, "1884 Report."
155. Richmond Exchange for Women's Work, "1885 By-laws."
156. Ibid.
157. Woman's Exchange, "1932 Report."
158. Dorothy Jones, *Sally Bell's Kitchen* (Richmond, 2001), 16.
159. *Richmond Times Dispatch*, April 6, 1980.
160. Jones, *Sally Bell's Kitchen*, 24–29.
161. Ibid., 33–35.
162. *Life Style*, November 1993.
163. Christophile Konstas and Nicole Lang, *Boxed Lunch*, 2013.
164. James Beard Foundation.

Chapter 17

165. Eliza Stickley Bristow, written personal memoir and interview with Virginia Randolph, located in archive at Virginia Randolph Museum, Glen Allen, Virginia.
166. Virginia Randolph, Jeanes Report, 1908.
167. 1930 U.S. Census.

168. Semmes McCormick,"Milestone in Life of Virginia Randolph: Henrico Educator Enters 55th Year as Teacher," *Richmond Times-Dispatch*, June 8, 1947.

169. *Richmond Times-Dispatch*, "Virginia Randolph," February 6, 1998.

170. Patty Kruszewski, "A Legacy of Learning," *Henrico Citizen*, May 5, 2011.

171. Kierner, Loux and Shockley, *Changing History*, 204.

172. Permanent exhibition, Virginia Randolph Museum, Glen Allen, Virginia.

173. Henrico County Television, "Virginia Estelle Randolph: Pioneer Educator," *Central Virginia Biographies*, October 16, 2009, henrico-va. granicus.com/MediaPlayer.php?publish_id=164.

174. United States, Freedman's Bank Records, 1865–74.

175. Kruszewski, "Legacy of Learning."

176. Henrico County Television, "Virginia Estelle Randolph."

177. Log cabin quilt on display, Virginia Randolph Museum, Glen Allen, Virginia.

178. Valinda Littlefield, "Jeanes Teachers: History, Goals and Duties, the Homemakers Clubs, Rosenwald Schools, Health Care, Contribution," education.stateuniversity.com/pages/2135/Jeanes-Teachers.html; Jones, *Jeanes Teacher*, 26.

179. Francis M. Foster Sr., "Richmond History: Miss Virginia Taught Beauty of Growth," *Richmond Times-Dispatch*, January 1, 2003, A-10.

180. McCormick, "Milestone in Life of Virginia Randolph."

181. Virginia Randolph, "A Brief Review of Work in Henrico County, Virginia, by First Jeanes Teacher," March 13, 1946.

182. *Richmond Times-Dispatch*, July 16, 1916.

183. Julian Houesman, "Virginia Randolph Lauded for Her Educational Feats," *Richmond News Leader*, May 16, 1940; Randolph, "Brief Review of Work."

184. *Richmond Times-Dispatch*, "Miss Randolph Dies: Was Pioneer Educator," March 17, 1958.

185. *Richmond Times-Dispatch*, "First Randolph Award Is Given to Senior," June 6, 1956.

186. Henrico County Television, "Virginia Estelle Randolph."

Chapter 18

187. Kierner and Treadway, *Virginia Women*, 185–87.

188. Sue Quinn, "Miss Ella G. Agnew Relates Story of Her Long, Active Career in Pioneer Field that Has Established Her as Virginia Leader in Rural, Home, Development," *Richmond Times-Dispatch*, October 20, 1944, 17.

189. Helen Ricks, "Virginia's Home Demonstration Leaders," *Southern Planter*, June 1948; Virginia Cooperative Extension, "4-H History," ext. vt.edu/4h-youth/history.html.

190. Betty Schmitz, "Home Demonstration Pioneer, Miss Agnew Recalls Early Days," *Richmond News Leader*, May 6, 1953.

191. Ella Graham Agnew, "The Story Covering the First Decade of Home Demonstration Work in Virginia, July 1, 1910–Jan. 1, 1920," Ella Agnew Papers, circa 1846–1992, Accession 42285, personal papers collection, Library of Virginia, 4.

192. Kierner and Treadway, *Virginia Women*, 186.

193. Quinn, "Miss Ella G. Agnew," 17.

194. Schmitz, "Home Demonstration Pioneer."

195. Agnew, "Story Covering the First Decade of Home Demonstration Work," 6.

196. Schmitz, "Home Demonstration Pioneer."

197. Frances Boushall, "Horse, Buggy Days Recalled by Home Agents," *Richmond News Leader*, May 9, 1946, 26.

198. Ibid.

199. Martha H. Swain and Helen Wolfe Evans, "Ella Graham Agnew (1871–1958)," *Dictionary of Virginia Biography*, Library of Virginia, 1998, www.lva.virginia.gov/public/dvb/bio.asp?b=Agnew_Ella_Graham.

200. "Virginia Home Economics Association News Letter, June 1947," Ella Agnew Papers, circa 1846-1992, Library of Virginia; Quinn, "Miss Ella G. Agnew," 17.

201. Quinn, "Miss Ella G. Agnew," 17.

202. Ibid.

203. "Virginia Home Economics Association News Letter, June 1947," Ella Agnew Papers, circa 1846–1992, Library of Virginia.

Chapter 19

204. Harry Kollatz Jr., "An Oasis of Refinement," *Richmond* magazine, November 2011, 207, 208.

205. Whitaker, *Tea at the Blue Lantern Inn*, 2–6.

206. U.S. Census 1910.

207. *Richmond Times-Dispatch*, "Boarding," November 28, 1911, 11.

208. *Richmond Times-Dispatch*, January 16, 1916, 56; *Richmond Times-Dispatch*, November 8, 1916, 4.

209. *Richmond Times-Dispatch*, "Professional Women to Hold Convention," June 27, 1919, 14.

210. Virginia League of Women Voters, *Virginia Cookery Book*, 1921.

211. *Richmond News Leader*, "Tearoom Founder's Rite Is Held," December 23, 1991, 23; Steve Clark, "People Want to Talk About Her Rolls, Not Her Politics," *Richmond News Leader*, April 22, 1982, 13.

212. Clark, "People Want to Talk About Her Rolls," 13.

213. Katherine Calos, "Last Patrons Toast Tearoom with Rolls," *Richmond News Leader*, July 17, 1991, 14.

214. Jann Malone, "Hot Roll Recipes Ease Loss of Mrs. Morton's Tea Room," *Richmond Times-Dispatch*, August 29, 1991, E-1.

Chapter 20

215. Brad Kutner, "Old Interbake Foods' Watertower Gets a 'Welcoming' Paint Job," *RVA mag*, October 10, 2016, rvamag.com/articles/full/26608/old-interbake-foods-watertower-gets-a-welcoming-paint.

216. Sandra Shelley, "Lofty Aspirations," *Virginia Living*, March 17, 2017, www.virginialiving.com/the-daily-post/lofty-aspirations.

217. Steve Row, "So the Cookie Won't Crumble: Interbake Foods Isn't Soft with Success," *Richmond News Leader*, December 18, 1989, B1–16.

218. *Times*, "Crackers by the Carload," March 7, 1900, 3.

219. *Times*, "Big Fire This Morning," May 23, 1900, 1.

220. Interbake, "Our History," www.interbake.com/recipe.

221. Interbake, "Timeline," www.interbake.com/our-history; National Register of Historic Places Registration Form, "Southern Biscuit Company," www.dhr.virginia.gov/registers/Cities/Richmond/127-6165_Southern_Biscuit_Company_2012_NR_FINAL.pdf.

222. Interbake, "Our History."

223. Row, "So the Cookie Won't Crumble."
224. Ames Arnold, "The Last FFVs," *Virginia Living*, October 2005, 72–73.
225. Row, "So the Cookie Won't Crumble."
226. Ibid.

Chapter 21

227. Kimball, *American City*, 40.
228. *The Land We Live In, the Land We Left*, www.virginiamemory.com/exhibitions/land_we_live_in/brochureLWLI.pdf.
229. Poplar Springs Baptist Church, "Our History," www.poplarspringsbc.com/About/OurHistory/tabid/63/Default.aspx.
230. National Archives and Records Administration (NARA), Washington, D.C., *Naturalization Petitions of the U.S. District Court for the Eastern District of Virginia (Richmond), 1906–1929*, Microfilm Roll *2*, Microfilm Serial *M1647*.
231. Steve Clark, "To Reach the Top, Ukrop Climbed Ladder to Catch Some Turkeys," *Richmond News Leader*, June 16, 1987.
232. Jenifer V. Buckman and Gregory J. Gilligan, "Grocery Patriarch Oversaw Expansion," *Richmond Times-Dispatch*, November 27, 2002, A-9.
233. Elliott Cooper "Ukrop, 34, Runs Growing Food Chain," *Richmond Times-Dispatch*, February 6, 1972, C-5.
234. Buckman and Gilligan, "Grocery Patriarch Oversaw Expansion," A-9.
235. Richard Foster, "Culture Meets Commerce," *Richmond* magazine, December 2011; Rich Griset, "How the Latino Vote Will Impact This Year's Election and the Future," *Chesterfield Observer*, October 12, 2016.

Chapter 22

236. Reynolds Foil, "Preparing Foods with Reynolds Wrap," 1950.
237. Reynolds Foil, "National Historic Landmark Application for Reynolds Foil HQ."
238. Arthur Hirsch, "Wrap It Up," *Baltimore Sun*, May 11, 1997.
239. Reynolds Foil, "Reynolds Review," 1950.
240. Richard S. Reynolds Foundation, "Our History," richardsreynoldsfoundation.org/history/the-company.
241. Reynolds Foil, "Aluminum and the Company that Makes It."

242. R.S. Reynolds, "Letter to W.S. Watts, President of Eskimo Pie Corp.," April 1, 1940.

243. Clarence Manning, "Letter to Fred Sunderhauf," April 25, 1944.

244. Hirsch, "Wrap It Up."

245. Reynolds Foil, "ABCs of Aluminum," 1955.

Chapter 23

246. "At the Counters," panel discussion at Fire, Flour & Fork, November 1, 2014.

247. Smartt, *Finding Thalhimers*, 163.

248. Peter Wallenstein, "The Richmond Sit-Ins," *Richmond Times-Dispatch*, February 21, 2010, E-1.

249. Smartt, *Finding Thalhimers*, 169.

250. Wallenstein, "Richmond Sit-Ins," E-1.

251. Christopher W. Schmidt, "The Sit-Ins and the State Action Doctrine," 18 Wm. & Mary Bill Rts. J. 767, (2010), scholarship.law.wm.edu/wmborj/vol18/iss3/6.

252. The New York Public Library's Schomburg Center for Research in Black Culture has digitized twenty-one volumes of the *Green-Books* from 1937 to 1964.

253. Wallenstein, *Blue Laws & Black Codes*, 116; Bonnie N. Davis, "'Richmond 32' Student Sit-in Commemorated with State Marker," *Richmond Free Press*, July 2, 2016, richmondfreepress.com/news/2016/jul/02/richmond-34-student-sit-commemorated-state-marker.

254. Harry Kollatz Jr., "Civil Disobedience," *Richmond* magazine, February 1, 2010, richmondmagazine.com/news/civil-disobedience-02-01-2010/.

255. Michael Paul Williams, "Elizabeth Johnson-Rice," *Richmond Times-Dispatch*, February 27, 2006, www.richmond.com/special-section/black-history/article_82824457-1292-551d-9d0e-b74b85d40a36.html.

256. Ibid.

257. Wallenstein, *Blue Laws & Black Codes*, 116.

258. Williams, "Elizabeth Johnson-Rice."

259. Kollatz, "Civil Disobedience."

260. Ibid.

261. Smartt, *Finding Thalhimers*, 162–63.

262. *Richmond News Leader*, "10 City Restaurants Desegregate Facilities," August 26, 1963.

263. *Richmond Times-Dispatch*, "Restaurants Here See Little Effect from Integration," August 3, 1963.
264. Cornell University, Legal Information Institute, "Civil Rights," www.law.cornell.edu/wex/civil_rights.

SELECTED BIBLIOGRAPHY

Alexander, Philip Bruce. *Virginia: Rebirth of the Old Dominion.* "Ellen Gertrude Tompkins Kidd: Biographical Sketch." Vol. 3. Chicago, 1929.

Berland, Kevin Joel, ed. *The Dividing Line Histories of William Byrd II of Westover.* Chapel Hill: University of North Carolina Press, 2013.

Beverly, Robert. *The History and Present State of Virginia.* Chapel Hill: University of North Carolina Press, 2013.

Bloom, Nicholas. *Merchant of Illusion: James Rouse, American's Salesman of the Businessman's Utopia.* Columbus: Ohio State University Press, 2004.

Burns, Brian. *Lewis Ginter: Richmond's Gilded Age Icon.* Charleston, SC: The History Press, 2011.

C.F. Sauer & Co. *Sauer's: A One Hundred Year History.* Richmond, VA: C.F. Sauer Co., 1987.

Dabney, Virginius. *Richmond: The Story of a City.* Charlottesville: University of Virginia Press, 1990.

Fuller, Andrew S. *The Grape Culturist: A Treatise on the Cultivation of the Native Grape.* New York: Orange Judd & Company, 1867.

Historic Richmond Foundation, Canal Committee. *Richmond's Historic Waterfront: Rockett's Landing to Tredegar, 1607–1865.* Richmond, VA: Historic Richmond Foundation, 1989.

Hylton, Patrick Evans. *Dishing Up Virginia: 145 Recipes that Celebrate Colonial Traditions and Contemporary Flavors.* North Adams, MA: Storey Publishing, 2013.

Jones, Lance G.E. *The Jeanes Teacher in the United States, 1908–1933: An Account of Twenty-Five Year's Experiences in the Supervision of Negro Rural Schools.* Chapel Hill: University of North Carolina Press, 1937.

Kierner, Cynthia A., and Sandra Gioia Treadway, eds. *Virginia Women, Their Lives and Times*. Vol. 2. Athens: University of Georgia Press, 2016.

Kierner, Cynthia A., Jennifer R. Loux and Megan Taylor Shockley. *Changing History: Virginia Women Through Four Centuries*. Richmond: Library of Virginia, 2013.

Kimball, Gregg. *American City, Southern Place: A Cultural History of Antebellum Richmond*. Athens: University of Georgia Press, 2000.

Kliman, Todd. *The Wild Vine: A Forgotten Grape and the Untold Story of American Wine*. N.p.: Broadway Paperbacks, 2010.

Kollatz, Harry, Jr. *True Richmond Stories*. Charleston, SC: The History Press, 2007.

Lankford, Nelson. *Richmond Burning*. New York: Penguin Books, 2003.

Manarin, Louis H., and Clifford Dowdey. *The History of Henrico County*. Richmond, VA, 2007.

McGraw, Marie Tyler. *At the Falls: Richmond, Virginia and Its People*. Chapel Hill: University of North Carolina Press, 1994.

Meacham, Sarah H. *Every Home a Distillery*. Baltimore, MD: Johns Hopkins University Press, 2009.

Miller, Adrian. *Soul Food: The Surprising Story of an American Cuisine, One Plate at a Time*. Chapel Hill: University of North Carolina Press, 2013.

Mordecai, Samuel. *Richmond in By-Gone Days*. Republished from the Second Edition of 1860. Richmond: Dietz Press, Inc., 1946.

Munford, George Wythe. *The Two Parsons*. Richmond: J.D.K. Sleight, 1884.

Potterfield, Tyler. *Nonesuch Place: Richmond Landscape*. Charleston, SC: The History Press, 2009.

Randolph, Mary. *The Virginia House-wife*. With historical notes and commentaries by Karen Hess. Columbia: University of South Carolina Press, 1984.

———. *The Virginia House-wife*. New York: Dover Edition, 1993.

Rountree, Helen. *The Powhatan Indians of Virginia*. Norman: University of Oklahoma Press, 1989.

Russell, Malinda. *A Domestic Cookbook: Containing Useful Receipts for the Kitchen*. N.p., 1866.

Schreiner, Ray. *Women Entrepreneurs of Richmond*. Richmond, 2009.

Scott, Mary Wingfield. *Old Richmond Neighborhoods*. Richmond: William Byrd Press, 1950.

Smartt, Elizabeth Thalhimer. *Finding Thalhimers: One Woman's Obsessive Quest for the True Story of Her Family and Their Beloved Department Store*. Manakin-Sabot, VA: Dementi Milestone, 2011.

Smith, John. *The Journals of Capt. John Smith: A Jamestown Biography.* Washington, D.C.: National Geographic Society, 2007.

Tyler, Lyon G. *Men of Mark in Virginia.* Vol 4. Washington, D.C.: Men of Mark Publishing Company, 1908.

————, ed. *Narratives of Early Virginia, 1606–1625.* New York: Charles Scribner's Sons, 1907.

Varon, Elizabeth. *Southern Lady, Yankee Spy.* New York: Oxford University Press, 2003.

Wallenstein, Peter. *Blue Laws & Black Codes.* Charlottesville: University of Virginia Press, 2004.

Whitaker, Jan. *Tea at the Blue Lantern Inn: A Social History of the Tea Craze in America.* New York: St. Martin's Press, 2002.

Wondrich, David. *Punch.* New York: Penguin, 2010.

Woodlief, Ann. *In River Time.* Chapel Hill, NC: Algonquin Books, 1985.

INDEX

ABOUT THE AUTHORS

Maureen Egan wrote *Insiders' Guide to Richmond, VA* for Globe Pequot Press in 2010. Since co-founding Real Richmond in 2010 with Susan Winiecki, Maureen has created numerous tours throughout Richmond's historic neighborhoods that showcase their culinary and cultural offerings to thousands of visitors and residents alike. In 2014, she and Susan produced Fire, Flour & Fork, an annual gathering for the food curious where dozens of engaging events relating to Richmond's culinary history and its contemporary vibrancy share the stage with some of the country's leading chefs, experts and authors. She was a longtime RHome columnist and board member of Friends of James River Park.

As editorial director of *Richmond* magazine and its sister publications, Susan Winiecki has been sharing the stories of the Richmond region, past and present, since 1996. A working journalist since high school, she has reported for small and large dailies and for morning news radio. She also has worked to create events that highlight the Richmond community, from the Theresa Pollak Awards for Excellence in the Arts to Broad Appetit, from the Elby Restaurant Awards to Fire, Flour & Fork. In 2010, she founded Real Richmond Food Tours with Maureen Egan, through which the Mid-Atlantic Food Writers Symposium was born. In 2013, Winiecki gave the welcoming address at the Southern Foodways Alliance Summer Symposium on Women and Food. She also received the Golden Trowel Award from Tricycle Gardens for her food-related community service work in 2014. She currently serves as board chair of Richmond Metropolitan Habitat for Humanity.

Visit us at
www.historypress.net